W9-CND-944

PERFECT PHRASES™

for

Healthcare Professionals

Hundreds of Ready-to-Use Phrases

Masashi Rotte, M.D.
Bernard Lopez, M.D.

New York   Chicago   San Francisco   Lisbon   London   Madrid   Mexico City
Milan   New Delhi   San Juan   Seoul   Singapore   Sydney   Toronto

The McGraw·Hill Companies

1 2 3 4 5 6 7 8 9 10 11 12 13 14 15   QFR/QFR   1 9 8 7 6 5 4 3 2 1

ISBN   978-0-07-176833-7
MHID   0-07-176833-5

e-ISBN 978-0-07-177345-4
e-MHID   0-07-177345-2

Library of Congress Cataloging-in-Publication Data

Rotte, Masashi.
        Perfect phrases for healthcare professionals : hundreds of ready-to-use phrases /
    by Masashi Rotte, Bernard Lopez.—1st ed.
            p. ;   cm.—(Perfect phrases series)
        ISBN-13: 978-0-07-176833-7 (pbk. : alk. paper)
        ISBN-10: 0-07-176833-5 (pbk. : alk. paper)
        I. Lopez, Bernard.   II. Title.   III. Series: Perfect phrases series.
        [DNLM: 1. Personnel, Hospital.   2. Professional-Patient Relations.
    3. Attitude of Health Personnel.   4. Communication.   5. Interprofessional
Relations. WX 160]

    LC classification not assigned
        610.69'6—dc23   2011033381

McGraw-Hill products are available at special quantity discounts to use as premiums and sales promotions or for use in corporate training programs. To contact a representative, please e-mail us at bulksales@mcgraw-hill.com.

This book is printed on acid-free paper.

Contents

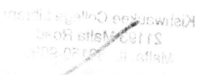

Preface

Medicine changes at a rapid pace, with new diseases being identified every year as well as new technologies and medications to provide medical care. It takes considerable time and energy just to keep up with the latest recommendations or medications. What does not change is the most fundamental part of healthcare—the relationships among people. These relationships exist among the caregiver and the patient and the patient's loved ones.

As healthcare providers, we are, in effect, given a sacred trust—to do what is best for our patients' health and well-being. Because we are involved in decisions that have significant effects on our patients' lives, we can become embroiled in areas of significant conflict. Sometimes, these conflicts are between us and our patients. Other times, these conflicts may involve the patient's loved ones or other healthcare professionals involved in the patient's care.

These conflicts often fall into two categories: dealing with difficult situations and dealing with difficult people. Difficult situations can range from giving patients bad news about their diagnosis to inquiring about the possibility of intimate partner violence. The gravity of these situations can make us or our patients feel uncomfortable.

Difficult people can be patients or their families who are angry about the outcome of care or who have unrealistic expectations. They may even be patients with psychiatric illnesses that distort their behavior around other people. It can also include our colleagues—doctors, nurses, and other healthcare providers—who are confrontational or rude at work. Unfortunately, difficult people are found in every field. Yet in healthcare, where the stakes and emotions can be very high, difficult and unpleasant interactions with patients or colleagues can have amplified significance.

This book is intended to help provide better care to patients by improving the communication between us and our patients. Having on hand a compendium of "stock phrases" for a range of complicated and potentially tense interactions can allow us, as health professionals, to expeditiously and effectively communicate with our patients, their families, and our colleagues. Improved communication between people in medical situations can lead to more efficient and satisfactory resolution of what can be life-and-death conflicts.

This book is not meant to replace or circumvent genuine interactions between patients and their caregivers or to cheapen human interactions to a list of generic stock phrases. It also cannot provide the insight or good judgment that comes with experience. It is meant to serve as a collection of strategies and a set of sample dialogues that we can draw upon to have better communication with our patients and colleagues.

Healthcare professionals include doctors, nurses, physician assistants, nurse practitioners, residents, and medical and nursing students. Hospital-based health professionals, such as Emergency Department doctors or nurses or occupational and physical therapists, only have contact with patients while they are in the hospital but not after discharge. Other providers, such as family doctors, may care for patients from birth to adulthood. The amount of trust and history built into these different types of relationships varies widely. What you take away from this book will depend on your job and your relationship with your patients.

Important Themes to Deal with Difficult Situations and Difficult People

■ Acknowledge and deal with conflicts as they arise. Dealing with difficult situations or people can be unpleasant and time consuming. Yet, putting off or glossing over conflicts or problems will not make the issue go away. If you sense a conflict, acknowledge it to the other party and try to deal with it as soon as it is appropriate. Don't allow conflicts to fester and become larger than they need to be.

■ Identify patients' expectations for their medical care. A common source of conflict is differing expectations between patients and their healthcare providers. A patient may expect that one prescription medication will permanently cure his or her high blood pressure and diabetes or that one surgery will end chronic back pain. At every patient encounter, try to explicitly identify patient expectations, and in return, give realistic goals for his or her care.

■ Introduce yourself to each person who is with the patient. Often, patients have loved ones with them at medical appointments. If you don't know who the other people with the patient are, it is beneficial to briefly introduce yourself to them. Be sure to identify the relationship between the patient and the other people. Some patients may have friends who are intimately aware of their medical problems, and the patients may want their friends in the room during all medical discussions. Other patients may have blood relatives with them but would prefer to consult with their healthcare provider in private.

Also, be aware that in contemporary society, many types of relationships exist among people. A male patient could be in a same-sex marriage and is being accompanied by his spouse. Even if a patient has a belief system that is different from your own, it is your duty to identify and respect your patient's beliefs.

■ Identify yourself and your role in the patient's care. Most patients are not aware of the role of the many different healthcare professionals they may encounter. During an outpatient office visit, a patient may give insurance information to a secretary, have vital signs measured by a nurse, be interviewed and examined by a medical student, and then be evaluated by a physician. The number of healthcare professionals a patient sees is amplified in other settings, such as in an Emergency Department or during a hospitalization. Patients can become overwhelmed and frustrated by the parade of people they see. It is important to let patients and their loved ones know who you are and the role you play in their care.

■ Don't use medical terminology with patients. When pressed for time, we, as healthcare professionals, can rush through conversations with patients and resort to using complex medical terms because this is how we communicate with other healthcare providers.

Taking a little extra time to use simple phrases and explaining difficult concepts can greatly help patients understand their conditions and have profound effects on our relationship with our patients.

■ Don't palm off responsibility to other providers. Deflecting blame for a problem onto another healthcare professional may seem like an easy way to get through difficult situations with patients. Yet, it does nothing for patient confidence in the medical field in general if you are "bad-mouthing" others involved in the patient's care. If you don't know the circumstances behind decisions that another healthcare professional has made, speak to that person directly rather than blame that person for the conflict at hand.

■ Always keep your cool. As healthcare professionals, we have the privilege to practice some of the most respected professions. We perform many important duties and should be proud of all of the hard work we did to reach our positions. Yet, there are times when patients or coworkers will behave in rude or even outrageous ways. You must maintain your professional demeanor at these times and not lose your "cool." Never let yourself descend to the level of yelling or using personal insults or vulgarities. This behavior diminishes your standing among your coworkers and does nothing to solve the conflict at hand.

Acknowledgments

The authors would like to thank the following individuals for their insights on communication between patients and healthcare professionals: Naisohn Arfai, M.D.; Yuan Liu; Rex Mathew, M.D.; Robert Perkel, M.D.; Joanna Rotte, Ph.D.; Steven Selbst, M.D.; Margaret Strosser; Michael Weinstein, M.D.; Mark Zwanger, M.D.; and Mischa Mirin, M.D.

About the Authors

Masashi Rotte, M.D., is a physician practicing emergency medicine at Thomas Jefferson University Hospital in Philadelphia, Pennsylvania. He has an interest in educating resident physicians and global health.

Bernard Lopez, M.D., is a physician practicing emergency medicine at Thomas Jefferson University Hospital in Philadelphia, Pennsylvania. He has an interest in educating resident physicians, medical students, and health-care providers in the practice of medicine.

Alan Forstater, M.D., is a physician practicing emergency medicine at Thomas Jefferson University Hospital in Philadelphia, Pennsylvania. He has an interest in professionalism and educating health-care providers about communications skills.

CHAPTER 1

Perfect Phrases for Patients Upset About Their Care

P eople have many different motivations for entering the field of healthcare. These motivations might range from an altruistic drive to help others to a desire to work in a job that is intellectually challenging. Still, we must remember that we are in a service industry—we get paid because we provide services to our patients, and they have a right to expect quality care from us.

There are myriad reasons that patients become upset about their care. More often than not, we have provided good care for our patients but factors beyond our control, such as insurance issues, wait times, or unrealistic patient expectations, obscure our hard work.

Perfect Phrases for Patients Upset About Wait Times

There are many steps in a medical encounter that force patients to wait for things to happen. In a typical outpatient office visit, patients can show up on time for an appointment but not see their provider for over an hour. Furthermore, wait times can vary widely, depending on the location of the office (urban versus suburban, academic medicine versus community medicine) and even the day of the week.

Patients can become quickly frustrated if they feel that they are waiting for no good reason. Whenever possible, let patients know upfront how long they should expect to wait and why they are waiting. This communication can be accomplished by something as simple as placing a sign in a waiting area or treatment room with expected wait times for office visits or procedures. If something does go wrong, such as a lab test being misplaced, explain this to the patient, apologize, and do your best to rectify the situation as quickly as possible.

Patients can also become angered when they see staff joking with each other, checking e-mail, or making personal phone calls. Patients seeing these behaviors may feel that they are being ignored and being made to wait unnecessarily. If you are on break or need to take care of some personal business, do it away from patient care areas so as to not appear indifferent to patient needs.

Mr. Smith is a patient who has come to the Emergency Department (ED) with ankle pain after a fall. He is upset

and complaining to the nurses and doctors because he has waited three hours to be seen.

When you enter a room to interview or examine a patient, be sure to introduce yourself and to explain your role in the patient's care. If the patient has other people in the room with him or her, be sure to identify their relationships to the patient.

→ Hello. I'm Dr. Gordon. I'm a doctor in the Emergency Department and I'll be responsible for your care here today. [To a woman sitting with the patient.] Are you here with Mr. Smith?

Apologize for their wait. If you were the patient, you wouldn't want to wait either.

→ I'm very sorry that you had to wait so long to be seen. We have not forgotten about you, but we are very busy today. We always make sure that each patient's problems are fully evaluated, and some problems take longer than others.

Acknowledge that you understand that the patient is upset, and then try to address his or her concerns. In addition, if your exam room allows it, sit down when you speak to patients. Studies have shown that when physicians interview their patients while sitting down and at eye level, patients overestimate the amount of time the physician was in the room with them.

→ I can see that you are upset about having to wait to be seen. You are right to expect to be treated quickly when you come to our hospital. Here is what I can try to do to get your x-rays done as soon as possible.

Emphasize to patients that you will do what is needed to take care of their medical problem.

→ I'm here to help you now and I'll spend as much time with you as you need.

Try to give patients periodic updates on the status of their care.

→ I just spoke with the radiology technician, and she is sending your films to the radiologist right now. We will try to get you out of here as soon as possible.

Mrs. Lee is waiting to see her dermatologist in the exam room of an outpatient office. She is having a follow-up visit after a skin biopsy. She is mad that her dermatologist hasn't been in to see her yet.

Letting patients know why they are waiting can often calm them down. If they realize that there are reasonable, or sometimes unavoidable, delays in their care, they may be more accepting of a wait.

→ I'm sorry that you have had to wait, but let me tell you the things we have been doing while you were waiting. I have reviewed your chart and the blood tests you had since our last visit. We also had to call the pathology lab because they had not sent over your results yet. In addition, my office staff had to contact your insurance company to verify your coverage. We have gotten all those things squared away, so now I'm here to focus on you.

Mr. Ford recently had a cardiac catheterization for chest pain. His cardiologist sent him to the ED because he has

swelling and pain in his groin where the catheter had been inserted into his femoral artery. He needs to have an ultrasound of his groin to make sure that he doesn't have an abscess or pseudoaneurysm. Unfortunately, it's a weekend night, and there is no ultrasound technician available until the morning.

If there is going to be a delay in some part of the patient's diagnostic or treatment plan, let him or her know about it up front, and explain the reason.

→ I just want you to know up front that we won't have an ultrasound technician here to do this test until the morning. I know it's a real hassle for you to have to wait this long, but I think this is a very important test.

If we explain the importance of tests or procedures, patients are often more accepting of delays.

→ There can be some serious causes of your symptoms, such as clots or damage to blood vessels. I want to make sure that we get the right diagnosis for your pain and swelling. Unfortunately, I can't make any decisions about your treatment plan until I get these test results.

Let the patient know what you can get done while he or she is waiting.

→ What I can do is call the radiology department so you are first on the list for testing tomorrow. While you are here overnight, we will give you all of the pain medicines you need and monitor you closely.

Mr. Hurwitz has presented to the Internal Medicine clinic at University Hospital to be evaluated for hypertension. He is complaining to the attending physician because a medical student and then a resident have interviewed and examined him.

According to the Association of American Medical Colleges, there were more than 1,000 teaching hospitals in the United States in 2009. Patients seen at teaching hospitals are cared for by medical students and residents.

→ *I'm tired of seeing you trainees. I want to see the real doctor. I don't want to have to keep repeating my medical history to the nurse and then the medical student and now some resident.*

Patients can become aggravated by having to undergo repeat interviews and physical exams. Nevertheless, performing a history and physical exam on numerous patients is essential to developing clinical skills. Let patients know that at a teaching hospital, they will see people at all levels of medical training.

→ I'm sorry you have had to repeat your medical history so many times. This is a teaching hospital, and that means that we have medical students and residents here, but we all work together. Sometimes, being seen by more than one person can help jog your memory or tease out some important details. I also want to emphasize that as the senior physician, I supervise all of your care.

Mr. Evans has had some pain in his abdomen after a cholecystectomy last week. He has come to his surgeon's office to be examined for the pain. The surgeon is in the operating

room, so the surgeon's nurse practitioner is evaluating the patient.

→ *Dr. Johnson operated on me, and I talked to her earlier today on the phone. She told me to come to the office. I only want Dr. Johnson to examine me.*

Patients may expect to see their physician at all office or inpatient visits. But because many physicians practice in groups or if they are indisposed, a patient may have to see a physician's partner or colleague. Let the patient know that your evaluation of them will be thorough and then communicated to his or her physician.

→ I work closely with Dr. Johnson. Unfortunately, she is taking care of a complicated case in the operating room and hasn't finished just yet. She asked me to come evaluate you, and anything you tell me I will be sure to relay to her. After I examine you, I will discuss your care with your surgeon, and we will come up with a plan for treating your pain.

Perfect Phrases for Patients Upset About Your Diagnostic or Treatment Plans

The diagnostic and treatment plan for a chief complaint should be tailored to each individual patient.

As healthcare professionals, we should suggest plans that we think are best for the patient. Nevertheless, patients have the right to choose other options and disagree with or question our reasoning. In turn, it is our right and duty to refuse to order tests or treatments that we feel offer no benefit or may harm a patient.

Many cases of disagreement over your diagnostic or treatment plans can be managed by educating the patient using plain words and offering the reasoning behind your decisions. It is also important to explicitly identify the patient's goals for his or her care as the patient may have very specific reasons for disagreeing with your plans.

Mr. O'Brien is a 65-year-old man who came to an outpatient clinic complaining of 10 days of diarrhea. You have decided to treat him for infectious diarrhea and have written him a prescription for an antibiotic. He is upset about something in his discharge paperwork and is demanding to speak to you.

→ *How come you wrote this prescription for me? It says on this paper that diarrhea is a side effect of this medication. I came here to get rid of my diarrhea, not get some medicine that is going to give me worse diarrhea. Do you know what you are doing?*

Patients may have incomplete or incorrect information about medications because they "saw something on the news" or had a friend that "had a bad experience with this drug." It is their right to question our medical decision making, and it is our duty to educate them about the treatment plans we offer them.

→ Diarrhea is a possible side effect of almost every antibiotic. But you are already having diarrhea, and I want to try something to help your situation. I chose this antibiotic for you because I think it will help your symptoms. I don't think it is very likely to make anything that is going on any worse.

→ *Are you a betting man? Because right now, all you are doing is gambling that I won't get diarrhea from these pills.*

Some patients are just plain rude people. In these cases, it is important to remain calm and professional and not take what they say personally. If you have made a reasonable and informed recommendation to a patient, stand by it. Sometimes, repeating or re-wording what you have already said can emphasize your point to a patient. Speak slowly and softly, and use layman's terms.

→ I hear your concerns. This antibiotic is one that I have prescribed many times for diarrhea. It is your body and your health we are talking about here, so the final decision as to whether or not to use this prescription is up to you. Nevertheless, I do think it will help your symptoms and make you feel better.

Mrs. Werth is a 25-year-old female who is at her primary care doctor's office. She works at a fast-food restaurant and is here today because she has had back pain since she fell at work while carrying a box. You have examined her and think her pain is due to a minor soft tissue injury.

→ *My manager told me that I need to get checked out since I fell at work. I need x-rays and an MRI (magnetic resonance imaging) of my back.*

→ I've examined you, and I haven't found anything that makes me concerned about a serious cause for your pain. I don't think x-rays or an MRI would give us any important information about your pain. I think you have bruising or a muscle strain and would benefit from some pain medicine and a few days of rest.

→ *Are you sure? My aunt had an MRI of her back and found she had some kind of serious problem. I really think I need an MRI.*

Oftentimes, patients are simply seeking reassurance regarding their symptoms. They may be afraid of a serious illness, and we can help them more by speaking with them than by ordering tests or medications.

→ You are right that an MRI is a good test for serious causes of back pain. But after speaking with you and performing a physical exam, I really don't think you have seriously injured your back at work. If you are still having back pain after a period of rest and pain medications, we could consider ordering you an MRI. Until then, let's try conservative therapy.

→ *All right. But I'm going to need at least a week off work. Can you write me a note?*

As healthcare professionals we should give patients medical excuse forms for a reasonable period of rest for their given injury. Giving a patient more than two to five days off for a minor soft tissue injury is unreasonable and is unlikely to be medically justified.

→ *I'm not able to give you more than three days off work. If you are still having serious symptoms after three days, you should come back to my office to be re-examined.*

Mrs. Sherman is a 42-year-old woman who has just slipped on the ice near your hospital and cut her cheek. It is 11 P.M. on a Saturday night, and she has presented to your ED. You have cleaned the wound and are preparing to suture it.

→ You are going to sew up my cut? But it's on my face. Aren't you just an Emergency Room (ER) doctor? I need a plastic surgeon to come in here and do it.

Acknowledge the patient's concerns, but clearly let her know that the treatment for her problem is within the scope of your practice.

→ I can tell that you are concerned about the appearance of any scars on your face. But I've done this kind of repair many times, and I'm confident I can close your wound very neatly.

→ *But this is on my face. I want a plastic surgeon.*

If a specialist is on call at your hospital, it may appease the patient to give him or her a call. You should let the specialist know that you are calling on the patient's insistence, in which case the specialist has the right to refuse to see the patient.

→ Let's do this to compromise. I'll call the plastic surgeon on call and tell her about your injury. I can't guarantee that she will come in, but I am willing to give her a call and tell her about your injury.

Perfect Phrases for Patients Upset About Outcomes of Their Care

Regardless of our intentions, almost all medical interventions, from medications to surgery, can have side effects or unintended consequences. Even if the medication or procedure improves the patient's condition, it may not be the outcome the patient wanted.

Mr. Roth had a benign lipoma removed from his arm two weeks ago. He is at his surgeon's office today and is not happy about the size of the scar on his arm at the excision site.

Patients should be given realistic expectations for their care. They should not be told that their new blood pressure pill will guarantee them perfect blood pressure or that their surgery will leave no scars if you aren't sure of it yourself.

→ I hear your concerns about the scar. Maybe I didn't do a good enough job letting you know what to expect after surgery. Let's talk about some things that can help promote wound healing.

Identifying a patient's expectations ahead of time can help a healthcare provider proactively address concerns. If the surgeon had asked the patient some of the following questions before the surgery, he might have known ahead of time that the patient had concerns about the cosmetic outcome.

→ We just spoke about the risks and benefits of this procedure. Do all the things I am telling you make sense? What questions about the procedure or recovery do you have for me?

Mr. Smith is a new patient to your practice. He has been living with Crohn's disease for several years and is seeing you today because he doesn't feel that his former doctor had been taking good care of him.

Don't try to palm off responsibility for a delay or bad outcome onto another healthcare provider. It is easy to blame someone else and deflect patient anger from you, but it doesn't make you or your organization look good. Making "grandstanding" comments about how poorly another provider cared for the patient serves only to raise unrealistic expectations for the job you will do.

→ That other doctor should have ordered a different test for you. They don't know what they are doing at that other hospital.

Instead, try to use measured but honest words about other providers.

→ I wasn't there when you had this test ordered, so I can't say exactly what the other doctor's plan was, and I can't speak for that doctor. In my opinion, the test I have ordered for you will be more useful for you than the one you have already had.

Patients must do their part for any medical intervention to be successful. We must educate patients regarding their role in their care and get them to invest in it. Ending the interaction with a review of the plan of care and the patient's role in that care can head off misunderstandings about outcomes.

→ Before we finish, let's quickly review what we have decided today. We will schedule you for a colonoscopy in two months and blood testing next month. We are going to start you on a new medicine. You are a vital part of your own care, and it is important that you take this medicine every day, as directed. Before we finish, what questions do you have for me?

Ms. Glaston is a 24-year-old woman who presented to the ED with one week of moderate, diffuse abdominal pain. She had a complete history and physical exam, laboratory testing, and an ultrasound of her pelvis and gallbladder. All of her testing is normal, and she is being discharged home with a diagnosis of "abdominal pain" and a prescription for an analgesic.

There are many times in medicine when we cannot find a definitive diagnosis for a patient's symptoms. The fact that we worked hard to rule out a serious or life-threatening condition may be lost on a patient.

→ *What do you mean you don't know what is causing my stomach to hurt? You did all these tests, and I waited for hours, and you don't know what is going on? Why did I even bother to come here?*

→ I'm sorry that you had to be here for a long time today. I wanted to make sure that you had a thorough workup and that we didn't miss anything. We also wanted to make sure that the medicines we gave you for pain had time to kick in.

Emphasize the positive aspects of the outcome of the patient's care.

Perfect Phrases for Patients Upset About Hospitalization

Some patients may be loath to be hospitalized, even if it is necessary to stabilize or treat their illnesses. Other patients will request admission to the hospital even if it isn't medically necessary or may refuse to be discharged. Patients will often have an underlying reason for their reluctance to be admitted or discharged. Identifying and addressing this reason can be vital to resolving conflicts over hospitalizations.

Mr. Shin is a 45-year-old man who presented to the ED with chest pain. The nurse practitioner treating him has recommended that he be admitted to the hospital for a cardiac stress test.

→ *You want me to stay here overnight? I've been here all day, and I'm sick of these tests. I just want to go home.*

→ My job is to give you my opinion on the best way to deal with your medical problem. You are in charge of your own health, so it's entirely up to you whether you want to take my advice.

We must respect patients' autonomy to make their own medical decisions, even if they are poor decisions. It is our job to give patients all of their diagnostic and treatment options and then advise them of what we think is the best course of action. If they do not wish to choose the options that we feel are in their best interest it is also our job to make sure that they understand the risks of their decisions.

→ The symptoms you described and your family's history of heart problems make me a little concerned about your heart. I strongly advise that you stay in the hospital for more testing. If you stay in the hospital, we can monitor your cardiac rhythms and can get you a stress test in the morning. If you go home and something goes wrong with your heart, we won't be there to help you. You could suffer damage to your heart, worsening pain, or even death.

It is important to ask this patient why he doesn't want to stay in the hospital. Perhaps he has a child he needs to take care of or he feels he cannot miss a day of work. Regardless, try to accommodate the patient's needs and wishes if it is in his medical interest. If the patient still makes what you feel is a poor choice, carefully document your discussion with the patient for your own protection.

→ I know it has been a long day and you have had a lot of tests. Is there something at home that you need to take care of? You can use this hospital phone if you need to call a family member or friend to help you out.

Mr. Johnson was sent to the ED after he presented to his family doctor's office with chest pain. An emergency physician and a cardiologist saw him. Both physicians feel that his chest pain is musculoskeletal in origin. They have informed him that he will be discharged home with pain medications and a recommendation for a few days of rest.

→ *You are sending me home? But I'm here to be admitted. My family doctor said that I should be admitted for cardiac testing.*

Physicians send patients to the ED for evaluation of complaints that can't be handled in the outpatient setting or after the office has closed. Patients may come with the expectation, possibly introduced by the physician who advised them to go to the ED, that they will be admitted or get certain tests right away. Yet, not all patients seen in the ED need to be admitted, nor do they need special testing, such as an MRI, on an emergent basis.

Let patients know, in simple terms, the reasoning behind your decision not to admit them. Get in touch with the physician or office that sent them to the ED. Offer reassurance about their symptoms and provide them with follow-up instructions. But if patients don't have a medical indication for admission, they should not be admitted even if they request it.

→ Your family doctor may have thought you needed to be admitted based on the conversation you had over the phone. But here, we've done a thorough evaluation of your heart, including blood tests, an ECG (electrocardiogram), and a chest x-ray. We also had a cardiologist come to see you. There really isn't anything else that we would do for you as an inpatient that we haven't already done.

→ *This doesn't make any sense. What am I supposed to do at home? What if my chest pain comes back!*

Acknowledge that the patient is concerned about his symptoms— even if you are not. If the patient seems upset about your plan to discharge him, ask him why and then address his specific concerns.

→ You may experience some pain at home, and that is why I will be providing you with a prescription for pain medicine. Is there anything in particular you are worried about that we haven't addressed?

→ *I just told you—my chest was hurting. Aren't you supposed to be a doctor? This could be a heart attack!*

Chest pain can be a sign of problems with your heart. But there are many other causes of chest pain that are not serious. Nothing that suggests a heart problem has shown up today on your physical exam or tests. The cardiologist has offered to see you in follow-up and can arrange for you to have a stress test in the near future.

Mr. DeSimone was hospitalized for debridement of a poorly healing leg wound that formed after an abscess was drained. His physician thinks he is ready to be discharged home. The patient is upset at the idea of being discharged and wants to stay in the hospital.

There is pressure from all sides to shorten or avoid hospitalizations for patients. Some of these pressures are financially driven and originate from insurance companies and hospital administrators. Yet, there are also medical reasons to shorten hospital stays, such as avoiding nosocomial infections or deep vein thrombosis.

→ Your leg wound is looking much better, and we think that you have improved to the point that we can discharge you so you can continue healing at home.

→ *I'm not ready to go home yet. My leg isn't healed enough.*

→ Your wound has improved a lot. The longer you are here in the hospital, the longer you are exposed to bacteria and viruses that other, sicker patients have. Your risk of getting an infection just from being in the hospital goes up every day you are here. You should also be more comfortable at home in your own bed.

→ *You just want me to leave the hospital because you want to save money and you know that I'm poor and don't have insurance.*

Patients may not want to be discharged home for many reasons. Some are based on secondary gain—patients may be homeless or have poor social circumstances and are simply more comfortable in the hospital. Other patients, such as the elderly or disabled, may be concerned that they won't be able to take care of themselves alone at home. If a patient is resisting discharge, ask what he or she is concerned about, and address those issues.

→ We treat all patients the same here regardless of their insurance status or ability to pay. Is there any specific reason you don't wish to be discharged? Are you worried about a problem at home or at work?

→ *I'm not going to be able to take care of myself—I can't walk on this leg.*

→ We have asked our social worker to help you set up for a home-care nurse to visit you once a day and clean out your wound. The social worker can also help you get a bedside commode so you won't have to walk to the bathroom. We will also provide you with prescriptions for antibiotics and medicines to treat pain.

Perfect Phrases for Patients Overwhelmed by the Number of Practitioners They Have Seen

Mrs. Jackson was recently hospitalized at an academic institution for abdominal pain due to diverticulitis. Several large abscesses were discovered upon imaging of her abdomen and pelvis. Her primary medical service has requested consults from the colorectal surgery and interventional radiology services to determine the best way to drain the abscesses. She was also seen by the gastrointestinal service and a social worker who is working on getting home nursing services for the patient after discharge. The primary medical team is making morning rounds on her.

Patients can be quickly overwhelmed by the number of people who see them during a hospitalization. A patient may be seen and treated by nurses, nursing assistants, medical students, residents, fellows, and attending physicians. A patient with complex medical problems will have a primary team and a number of specialists caring for them. They may also be whisked out of their rooms frequently for procedures or surgeries.

→ *I've seen six different doctors since last night—I don't know who anyone is anymore.*

Most patients are not aware of the roles of the many different healthcare professionals they may encounter. Patients can become frustrated by the parade of people they see. It is important to clearly let the patient and his or her loved ones know who you are and the role you play in their care.

→ We have asked the GI (gastrointestinal) doctors and the colorectal surgeons to evaluate you in the event that you need surgery while you are here in the hospital. I know it can be confusing to see so many people, but we will be your primary medical team while you are here. We are the "quarterback" for your care and coordinate all the different people who are working hard to get you better.

Patients may benefit from a list of the services that are providing care for them. Offer patients a pad of paper to write down your name and role in their care.

Perfect Phrases for Issues Related to the Care of Pediatric Patients

Caring for pediatric patients can be stressful for healthcare professionals. The "stakes" are higher when caring for children, and thus, each and every medical decision can carry added weight. In addition, when treating children, you have to deal with two "patients"—the child and the parents. The style of parenting and the role the parents take in their child's life can help or hinder the care of the pediatric patient.

When evaluating children, try to sit down and interview them at their eye level. If they can speak, involve them in the discussion about their medical problems. The child may not be able to answer your questions, but engaging the child lets the parents know that you care about their child's health.

Daniel is a 3-year-old boy, who has been brought to the ED by his parents. He has had three days of vomiting and diarrhea. You have examined the child and feel that he needs some blood chemistry tests and intravenous hydration.

Parents are their children's strongest advocates. For some parents, that may mean that they are fiercely against any and all testing or treatment that may cause their child pain.

→ *Hold on a second. I don't want anyone getting near Daniel with a needle. He hates needles, and I don't want him to be tortured. We just want to get him some medicine for his throwing up and diarrhea, and then we will go home.*

It is important to acknowledge that the parents are doing what they think is best for their child. In turn, emphasize that you, as a healthcare professional, want what is best for the patient. Explain, in simple words, why you think the patient needs the tests or treatments.

→ I hear your concerns, and I can tell that you care deeply about your son. We don't want to him to suffer either. But his symptoms and physical exam findings are a little concerning, and I think he looks dehydrated. We will put in a very small IV to try to minimize pain. Again, we are only suggesting these tests and the IV because we care about your son's health, too.

→ *Isn't there anything else you can do besides a needle? I just know he is going to suffer.*

Ultimately, all medical decisions go through the parents. Some will not allow you to do what you think is best for the child. In that case, you must respect their wishes but ensure that you document in the medical record your reasoning and discussion with the parents.

→ You are Daniel's parent, so all the medical decisions are up to you. We can't force anything on you or him. But at this point, I do believe he needs to have the tests and IV done.

In contrast to the parent in the above scenario, some parents may not be satisfied that their child is being thoroughly cared for until every test has been exhausted.

→　*What kind of blood tests are you going to do? Can you give her some antibiotics? I want to make sure she gets completely checked out. Could this be appendicitis? Does she need an MRI?*

Again, acknowledge that such parents are doing what they think is best for their children. As healthcare professionals, it is our job to educate our patients.

→　I know you only want what is best for Helen. We do, too. But ordering extra tests or medications won't help her out at this point. I'm willing and able to get Helen any tests or medications she needs, but right now, I think it would be best to start out with some basic tests. If anything abnormal shows up, we can order additional tests, as needed.

Samuel is a 14-year-old boy with asthma, who has presented to his pediatrician's office with wheezing, fever, and chest pain. You have examined the child and think he needs a chest x-ray to rule out pneumonia.

There is an increased awareness and concern in the medical community about the amount of ionizing radiation to which our patients are being exposed. This is an especially valid concern among pediatric patients, as they have a longer life span, during which they can develop complications from radiation exposure. Parents can be keenly aware of the long-term side effects of radiation and may question your reasoning behind radiologic imaging tests.

→　*Why do you think Samuel needs this chest x-ray? I read online that x-rays can cause cancer. Are you sure he needs this test?*

Educating patients and families about the risks and benefits of radiographic tests and also ensuring that we only order tests our patients actually need are vital to providing good care.

→ You have brought up a valid point, and I'll be happy to address it. I think Samuel needs an x-ray because he may have pneumonia. If he does have pneumonia, it will change the way we treat his symptoms. X-rays do expose patients to radiation, and you are correct in thinking that it could lead to cancer. But one chest x-ray will expose him to a very small amount of radiation, and this amount is nowhere near enough to cause cancer. In fact, studies have shown that Samuel would need hundreds, if not thousands, of chest x-rays before he got a cancer-causing amount of radiation. So, in this case, the benefits of properly diagnosing pneumonia outweigh the very small risks.

Michelle is an 8-year-old girl admitted to the hospital from her pediatrician's office with fever, headache, and neck pain. The inpatient pediatrician feels that Michelle needs a lumbar puncture to rule out meningitis. The pediatrician has brought a consent form and a lumbar puncture kit to the patient's room.

→ *You are going to do the spinal tap? I thought only neurologists do those. Can't you go get a neurologist?*

Parents can be vocal about any aspect of their children's care that is not meeting their expectations. Don't take their concerns personally; rather, listen to what they have to say, and respond to it. In this case, the inpatient pediatrician is competent to perform this procedure. Reassure the parent by confidently stating the risks and benefits of the procedure and also your experience level with it.

→ Many types of doctors, including pediatricians, perform lumbar punctures. It's an important test when we are concerned about meningitis. I've done this procedure many times, and I am confident that I can do it quickly and will minimize any pain that it causes Michelle.

CHAPTER 2

Perfect Phrases for Patients Suffering from a Medical Error

Errors are more common in medicine than healthcare professionals would like to believe. The 1999 report from the Institute of Medicine entitled "To Err Is Human" showed that there are between 44,000 and 98,000 preventable deaths and more than one million injuries each year due to medical errors. This report defined a *medical error* as the "failure of a planned action to be completed as intended or the use of a wrong plan to achieve an aim."

Patients who have suffered from a medical error have a right to know what has happened to them and why. Multiple organizations, such as the National Patient Safety Foundation and the Joint Commission on Accreditation of Healthcare Organizations, endorse open communication about medical errors. Disclosing an error can be a challenge for healthcare professionals. We are driven people with high expectations for ourselves and have worked very hard to get to our current positions. Admitting that we made a mistake forces us to face a range of fears.

One fear is that our patients will become angry with us or lose trust in our care and that this might damage the relationship going forward. We may also be afraid that our patients, with the knowledge that a mistake was made, will pursue legal action against us. We are also afraid of facing our egos—as accomplished people, admitting a mistake can damage our concept of our own infallibility and make us afraid that our peers will lose respect for us.

Why Should Medical Errors Be Disclosed?

There are multiple reasons why medical errors should be disclosed to patients. Patients are placing their bodies and health in our hands. They have a right to know if they have been harmed by a medical error. This disclosure allows patients to understand why they may have had an unfavorable outcome from a medical intervention. This information can then help them make informed decisions about their future care. Patients may also deserve compensation for the untoward outcomes of a medical error; disclosure allows them to pursue this compensation.

What Are the Risks and Benefits of Error Disclosure?

There are definite risks associated with disclosing medical errors. One risk is that the disclosure could incite a patient or his or her family to file a malpractice lawsuit. Another risk is that by admitting to making a mistake could jeopardize the patient's trust in your clinical skills and undermine your relationship with the patient.

Nevertheless, there are benefits to error disclosure. Some patients file lawsuits to gain access to information that they feel is being withheld about what went wrong with their care. By providing full disclosure of errors up front in a caring and sensitive manner, potential lawsuits can be headed off. Large studies at the University of Michigan Health System and the Veteran's Administration demonstrated that error disclosure programs that they instituted at their hospitals actually decreased the number of malpractice lawsuits and their associated monetary outlay.

Error disclosure can sometimes improve your relationship with your patients because they see firsthand that you are being honest with them and have their best interests at heart. If a case does go to trial, and errors that result in severe harm to the patient may end up in court regardless, a documented error disclosure and apology in the medical record is only to your benefit.

Which Medical Errors Should Be Disclosed?

It is not prudent or practical to disclose all medical errors to patients. Errors that are very minor and have no lasting or deleterious effects on a patient do not always need to be disclosed. For instance, if an ankle x-ray was ordered on the left side but was performed on both the right and left sides, there is no harm to the patient—the patient was exposed to a negligible amount of radiation. In this case, the patient may not even notice or care that he or she had an unnecessary x-ray. Errors resulting in definite harm, such as a patient being given the wrong dose of medication that results in serious injury or death, should always be disclosed.

A number of medical errors fall into a category where we can't always be sure that the error itself led to actual harm. An example is a lab or x-ray finding that was abnormal but was overlooked by the patient's treatment team. If the patient has a poor outcome, it is often very hard to determine if that missed lab or imaging test would have altered the patient's care or outcome in any way. It can be very challenging to decide whether or not to disclose these types of errors.

The American College of Physicians recommends telling patients about "procedural or judgment errors made in the course of care if such information is material to the patient's well-being." However, there are no measurements or calculations that can guide disclosure in these "gray areas." In these situations, you must rely on your best clinical judgment to determine if the error had any actual clinical significance and gauge the risk/benefit ratio of error disclosure. One way to make this decision is to ask yourself, "What would I like to know if my family member were the patient in this situation?"

How Should a Medical Error Be Disclosed?

It is important to have a plan laid out ahead of time for disclosing an error to a patient and his or her family, as well as some prepared phrases in mind. Thinking through the following questions ahead of time will allow you to prepare a "game plan" for this difficult meeting.

■ **Who will be present for the meeting and who will lead the disclosure?** The patient's attending physician should always be present, even if the error was not on his or her part. If a resident physician or a nurse committed the error, they should be there as well, although they might not necessarily lead the discussion. A nurse manager or social worker may provide emotional support for the patient and family. After the meeting, document in the medical record who was at the meeting and an overview of what was said.

■ **When should it occur?** Ideally, error disclosure should take place within 24 hours of its discovery. However, you must pick the right place and time to disclose an error. Patients recovering from anesthesia will not be in the right state of mind to understand what you are telling them. A family that has just learned that their loved one has died probably needs at least a few hours to emotionally process the news before you give them more information. Additionally, take the time you need to be reasonably certain that an error actually occurred and that the injury to the patient was the result of the error. Having a long and tense discussion with a patient when something wasn't actually your fault benefits no one.

■ **What should be said in the meeting?** The purpose of the meeting is to share, to the best of your knowledge, what happened to the patient and why. Give the patient a brief summary of what the error was, what the consequences of the error are, how these consequences can be corrected or mitigated, and how you will try to prevent this error in the future. Undoubtedly, the patient will have many questions about what you are telling him or her. If you aren't sure of the answers to these questions, do not fabricate or guess at answers. Rather, let the patient know that you will try to find out the answers and get back as soon as possible.

It is vital that this conversation be conducted in a caring and empathetic manner. If the facts surrounding the error are still in doubt, an expression of empathy for the patient's plight in general may be sufficient until more is known. Finally, close the meeting with an apology. Although some patients may surprise you by their graciousness and understanding, others may be distrustful or even angry. Try to prepare for a variety of emotions, perhaps in many combinations and at various times. A patient may even ask for another physician to assume his or her care going forward.

Preventing Errors in the First Place

The process of diagnosing and treating disease is incredibly complex, and there are many areas where errors can be introduced. Healthcare professionals should learn from the mistakes of others and anticipate the following potential problem areas:

■ **Sign out**—There is a major potential for lapses in patient care when responsibility for a patient is transferred from one physician to another or from one nurse to another. It is your job as a healthcare professional to make sure that you are giving the pertinent facts to the next provider. If you are getting the sign-out, you must also make sure that you have all the information you need to take over the patient's care. Some institutions have standardized sign-out procedure or even forms that must be adhered to in order to ensure the safe hand-off of patients.

■ **Medication ordering**—Prescription of medications is the most common cause of medical error. Being vigilant to check for drug interactions, double-checking dosages and transcribing orders legibly can head off potential problems before they occur. Always record pediatric weight in kilograms rather than pounds, never use medication abbreviations that could be misinterpreted, and, if possible, use an electronic ordering system that can automatically check for interactions. In addition, pharmacists and nursing staff should be actively involved in checking for medication ordering errors.

■ **Procedure verification**—Adopting a mandatory checklist or "time-out" before performing invasive procedures can help reduce errors such as wrong-site surgeries. Having all team members identify themselves and their roles in the procedure during the "time-out" will make it more likely that one of them will speak up if he or she sees an error.

Even when we try our hardest, errors will still occur. Having a system in place to review errors can give valuable insight into how the error occurred and if there are individual or system problems that need to be addressed. Large institutions usually have morbidity and mortality conferences, and patient safety or risk management offices that serve this function. In smaller or solo practices, a weekly conference may not be practical, but regularly conducting an honest and thorough review of errors may help prevent future errors.

Perfect Phrases for Examples of Error Disclosure

Mr. Hammond was admitted to the hospital for intravenous antibiotics to treat a wound infection he had developed after a routine operation. The patient had a known allergy to penicillin, but the overnight resident mistakenly ordered for piperacillin and tazobactam, a penicillin-based medication. The patient developed hives, and felt like his throat was closing up shortly after he was administered the medication. He received intravenous steroids and diphenhydramine, and his symptoms remitted after 30 minutes.

This error lies squarely on the shoulders of the resident who ordered the wrong medication. However, this hospital should have a system of checks and balances in place to detect and prevent medication errors. A computerized order system or strict double-checking of orders by a pharmacist and nurse may have prevented this error.

Thankfully, the patient suffered no harm due to the error. But surely, this patient did notice that he had some type of reaction to a medication. He should therefore be made aware of the error, and an apology is in order. The attending physician and the resident should plan to meet with the patient. This meeting does not necessarily need to occur overnight but should be done early the next day, perhaps during rounds. Before the meeting, the attending and resident should discuss what happened and why, and they should briefly go over what will be said during the meeting with the patient.

➜   Mr. Hammond, overnight you developed hives and felt like your throat was closing up shortly after you were given some intravenous (IV) antibiotics. I need to tell you that you had that reaction because you were mistakenly given a penicillin-based antibiotic.

Let the patient know, to the best of your ability, why the error occurred and what will be done to address any medical consequences.

→ I've talked about this with the resident who was caring for you overnight, and it seems that he overlooked your allergy to penicillin. To make sure that your allergic reaction didn't get any worse, we gave you some medicines to head off the reaction, and we are going to monitor you closely for the rest of your hospital stay. We've also changed your medications to a non–penicillin-based antibiotic. I don't anticipate that you will suffer any long-term injury as a result of this reaction.

Apologize to the patient, and let him or her know what steps will be taken to prevent similar errors in the future. However, don't promise changes that you aren't positive will occur. If you aren't sure that a task force will study this error and make recommendations to adjust hospital policies, don't tell the patient that one is to be convened shortly.

→ I am very sorry that this happened. I'm sure that having hives and feeling like your throat was closing were terrible experiences. I've had a personal discussion with my resident about the importance of medication allergies, and I've notified your nursing staff to be extra vigilant about your medication allergies. I'm also going to bring up this error at the next faculty meeting so that we can determine if we should have some new policies put in place in the hospital.

How much of a role the resident takes in this discussion depends on the situation and people involved. In this case, the resident offering an apology to the patient would probably be an important gesture. In closing, make sure the patient knows that his or her health is the paramount consideration.

➜ Mr. Hammond, I also want to apologize for what happened. I feel awful that I made this mistake. I hope that it will be all right with you if I am still part of the team caring for you in the hospital. I am glad to see that you are doing well this morning, and I want you to know that I am going to work hard to make sure that you get better.

Mr. Feldheim is in your office for his annual checkup. He has had the results of a panel of screening labs and the interpretation of a routine chest x-ray sent to your office. You notice that his chest x-ray shows a 1.5-cm pulmonary nodule. You review his chest x-ray from one year ago and notice that the prior report noted a 1.1-cm nodule. You cannot remember if you discussed this nodule with the patient last year and have no record of a discussion.

Abnormal lab or imaging findings and their implications should be discussed with patients in a timely manner. It seems that this abnormality was not brought to the patient's attention last year. In the interim, the nodule has grown. This clinical significance of this oversight depends on several factors, such as the patient's risk factors for lung cancer. Nevertheless, this is a result that was overlooked for one year and has subsequently changed; the patient should be made aware of this error.

→ Mr. Feldheim, I need to discuss a finding on your chest x-ray. You have a small pulmonary nodule in the middle part of your right lung. I looked at last year's chest x-ray, and this nodule was there last year as well but it has slightly increased in size since then. I honestly cannot remember if we discussed this nodule after your x-ray. I fear that I may have overlooked this result by accident last year. I am very sorry for this oversight.

Tell the patient what you think the clinical significance of the error is and how going forward you can deal with any consequences of the error.

→ A pulmonary nodule is a small growth in the lung. You aren't a smoker and are healthy otherwise. So, I think it is likely that this nodule is not a serious problem like cancer. But I think that we do need to get a CT (computed tomography) scan of your chest as soon as possible to make sure that this is nothing serious. I am also going to call a colleague who is a lung specialist and get you an appointment to see her right away.

Let the patient know what you can do to prevent similar errors in the future. Close with an apology, and always give the patient the opportunity to ask questions.

→ I am going to talk about this oversight with my office manager today to try to figure out why I missed last year's report. I take responsibility for this error. You have been my patient for several years now, and I appreciate your letting me take care of you. I want you to know how sorry I am. What questions do you have for me?

Mr. Smith was having an operation to resect a cancerous mass from his descending colon. During the operation, the surgeon accidentally lacerated the patient's ureter. Because of the damage to the ureter, a urologist had to be called into the case to repair the injury. The surgeon is now at the patient's bedside in the recovery room to discuss the error.

Make sure that the patient or a family member is able to understand what you are going to tell them. In the immediate post-operative period, a patient will likely still be under the effects of anesthesia and not competent enough to understand what you are going to tell them. Sit down to speak to the patient and family at eye level, and use plain language.

➜ This is very hard for me to tell you because we have been working hard to get the best outcome for your cancer resection. Unfortunately, there was an injury to one of your ureters during the surgery. This is a small tube that carries urine from the kidneys to the bladder. It lies near the part of the colon I was operating on, and I must have accidentally cut it while I was working on the colon.

Describe what you did to fix the error.

➜ As soon as I noticed the injury, I called one of our best urologic surgeons, Dr. Singh, to come into the operating room and repair the ureter. Fortunately, Dr. Singh was able to place a small stent into the ureter to keep it open and then fixed the injury. He will come and check on your stent tomorrow morning.

Discuss what can be done to help prevent the error in the future.

➜ I want to make sure that this type of injury doesn't occur to future patients of our hospital. I plan to meet with the other surgeons in our hospital and see what steps we can take in the operating room to prevent this type of injury in the future. I'm going to make sure that you are kept well informed of any complications arising from the injury to your ureter.

This error is unlikely to cause this patient any permanent or serious injury. However, it may be prudent to notify your hospital's risk management office before disclosing this error to the patient. Regardless, clearly document in the chart the date, time, and place of the error disclosure as well as who was present and what was said.

Offering an apology for a medical error is an important part of error disclosure. Yet, there is an entirely reasonable concern that apologizing for a patient's outcome, whether it was due to a medical error or was simply the natural course of the underlying disease, could be interpreted as admission of guilt. Consequently, the majority of states have enacted laws that exclude the words used to apologize or express grief from being used in court against the physician, if the incident goes to trial in a medical malpractice case.

➜ I want you to know that I am sorry that you had this complication during an otherwise successful surgery. I am confident that you won't suffer any long-term damage going forward.

Effect of Error on the Healthcare Professional

A medical error can have devastating consequences for a patient, but it can also have an impact on the healthcare professional who committed the error. Most of us went into the field of medicine to help patients; knowing that our mistake caused harm to a patient can lead to feelings of guilt or incompetence.

Our thoughts may dwell on the events surrounding the error and their effect on our relationship with the patient and his or her family. Our confidence in our abilities as healthcare providers may be undermined, and that can, in turn, alter our decision-making process when we take care of other patients. We may worry that our colleagues will lose respect for us or that a lawsuit is quickly taking shape against us. Some healthcare professionals have become clinically depressed, quit the profession, or even harmed themselves because of these feelings.

These intense emotions and their associated untoward effects have been termed the *second victim phenomenon*. Consider getting help if you are ever in this position. If you work for a hospital, see if there are resources or support for you to turn to. In a group or solo practice, you may need to turn to a trusted colleague or even a psychiatrist for help to get through this tough period.

CHAPTER 3

Perfect Phrases for Patients Wanting Medically Unnecessary Prescriptions or Tests

P atients may approach medical care with strong expectations that they will be prescribed certain types of testing or treatments. These expectations arise from a variety of sources. One compelling source is having seen family or friends undergo treatment for similar medical conditions. Another is the depiction of modern medicine on television and film. These media depictions, although often unrealistic, can be powerful to people without medical training. In addition, there is a preponderance of direct marketing of medications, medical devices, and services to consumers. No one can open a magazine, turn on the television, or browse the Internet without running into an advertisement for a new drug or a local hospital's gastric bypass surgery suite.

As a result of these influences, patients often ask for certain medications by name or request that certain testing be performed (e.g., magnetic resonance imaging [MRI] for knee pain or invasive cardiac testing for chest pain). On the one hand, it is important for patients to take an active part in their medical care by engaging their healthcare providers. By questioning the rationale for medical decisions, patients become more informed and therefore more invested in their own care. On the other hand, patients are not always aware of the risks, benefits, side effects, and costs of the care they are requesting. It is our job as healthcare professionals to educate patients about what we think is the best way to diagnose and treat their ailments. That may mean that we recommend simpler diagnostic testing before moving on to more invasive and expensive testing or a generic medication instead of the latest name brand pill.

When we make these recommendations, patients may imagine that we do not have their best interests at heart because we aren't satisfying their preconceived expectations of treatment. As healthcare professionals, we need to be able to effectively communicate to patients why we are making the recommendations while still maintaining a strong and trusting relationship with patients and their families.

Perfect Phrases for Patients Requesting Unnecessary or Inappropriate Medications

Mrs. Johnson is at her doctor's office and is requesting a new medicine for blood pressure that she saw advertised on television. She thinks that the new medicine will work better than her current ones. You (as her doctor, nurse practitioner, or physician's assistant) don't feel, on the basis of current studies, that the new drug works better, even though it costs five times as much as her current medications.

→ I think it's great that you are paying close attention to your high blood pressure. I also want to make sure that your blood pressure is well controlled.

This patient is clearly invested in her care and is engaging her healthcare provider to ensure that she gets the best care possible. Not all patients pay attention to their chronic diseases, so this patient should be appreciated and encouraged to continue managing her disease.

→ I, too, have seen the advertisements for this new medicine, but at this point I don't think the new medicine has proven to be more effective than our current options. Here are the adjustments to your current medications that we can try to better control your blood pressure.

Direct-to-consumer advertising (DTCA) can play a powerful role in which medications patients request. According to the Nielsen Company, in 2008, pharmaceutical companies spent more than $4.3 billion in the United States alone on DTCA for prescription drugs. The only industry spending more on DTCA was the automobile industry. As healthcare professionals, we should recognize the influence that DTCA can have on patient requests. If an expensive, brand name medication is not medically necessary, explain this situation clearly to the patient and encourage him or her to try a less expensive generic medicine.

Elizabeth is a 20-year-old college student who has visited a psychiatrist's office for help with her mood swings and fatigue. After interviewing the patient, the psychiatrist thinks she may have bipolar disorder and suggests a mood stabilizing medication. The patient reacts angrily to this suggestion.

➜ *I don't know what you are talking about—I need you to write me a prescription for Zoloft because I have generalized anxiety disorder.*

This patient clearly feels that she has a specific disorder. Ask explicit questions to find out why the patient feels that way and what she wants or expects of you as her healthcare provider.

➜ Why do you think you have generalized anxiety disorder? How did you hear about Zoloft?

➜ *I saw an ad in a magazine I read.*

➜ What about this ad hit home for you?

➜ *Well, the ad mentioned symptoms such as fatigue, anxiousness, mood swings, and irritability. I feel like I have all those symptoms, so I must have generalized anxiety disorder. Why don't you think I should get Zoloft?*

In this patient's case, the patient has strongly identified her somatic and psychiatric symptoms with the advertising for the name brand medication. Acknowledge the patient's concerns and her perception of her problem.

→ I see where you are coming from, and I'm glad that you have come in to my office to get some help. I agree with you that your symptoms may be due to a psychiatric condition. I'm just not sure that the condition is actually generalized anxiety disorder. I would like to check a few blood tests and try you on another medication first. If it does not work for you, I will be happy to revisit this issue.

Mr. Sanchez is at his surgeon's office and is being seen in follow-up for a minor leg surgery. While there, he asks the surgeon for a prescription for refills for his hypertension and diabetes medications.

→ The incision on your leg is healing well. As for these medications, I think it would be better if you saw your family doctor to get prescriptions if they aren't related to your surgery.

→ *Come on, doc. Can't you just write me a prescription for these medications? I have to make another appointment with my family doctor, and I'm already here. You are a doctor. All you have to do is pick up a pen.*

In this case, the patient is requesting medications that are medically necessary for his medical problems. But it is not appropriate for the surgeon to refill these medications. The patient's primary care provider should be coordinating all of his care. Specialists or consultants may choose to prescribe medications related to the condition they are treating, but refills or adjustments to other medications should be left to the physician who originally wrote the prescription.

→ It would be better for you to see your primary care doctor to get these medications. Your family doctor may want to adjust your medications or do some routine blood testing to check up on your diabetes. I'm sorry that you will have to take time out of your schedule for another appointment, but I think it's better for you in the long run.

Mr. Shah has made a sick visit appointment at his family doctor's office. He has had three to four days of muscle aches, fatigue, and rhinorrhea. The physician assistant who is evaluating him has diagnosed him with a viral upper respiratory infection (URI).

→ *I think I need some antibiotics. The last time I had something like this I took some pills, and it went right away.*

It is a common misconception that a URI should be treated with antibiotics. Educating our patients about this medical myth and others is an important part of our role as healthcare professionals.

→ I think that what you have is a cold—we know that viruses cause almost all colds. Antibiotics don't work on viruses. They only work on bacterial infections, so I don't think a prescription for antibiotics will help you get better.

→ *But I'm tired of feeling sick. I really think some antibiotics will help.*

→ I'm sure you are sick of feeling achy and having a stuffy head. But again, antibiotics are not likely to help your situation. I think you will start to feel better in a few days regardless of whether or not I prescribe you antibiotics. There are also some potential downsides to antibiotics, such as stomach upset and diarrhea. I suggest we treat you with some pain medications, decongestants, and a few days of rest.

A reasonable explanation using simple words regarding why you don't recommend antibiotics can dissuade some patients from requesting unnecessary prescriptions. Yet, other patients may be insistent that you write them prescriptions for antibiotics. As healthcare professionals, we are never obligated to write a prescription if we don't think the patient needs it or if it may harm the patient.

Nevertheless, you have to pick and choose your battles. Convincing a patient to forgo an unnecessary prescription may take an inordinate amount of your time or may jeopardize your relationship with the patient. If the patient is absolutely insistent on a prescription for a short course of antibiotics, which has a low risk of any serious side effects, it is within your discretion to relent. It is our job to make sure that our patients are informed about the risks and benefits of medical interventions. Patients do have the right to make decisions about their own care, even if the decisions are unwise.

→ *A decongestant and rest aren't going to work. I really NEED some antibiotics.*

→ OK. I can write you a prescription for a short course of pills. I want to emphasize that I don't think this is the best thing for you. But you have been our patient here at the clinic for a long time, and we want you to be happy and healthy.

Mr. Lange has brought Leela, his 5-year-old daughter, to the pediatrician's office for a sick visit. The girl has had three days of runny nose and intermittent low-grade fever. The pediatrician has examined the patient and feels that she has a viral URI.

→ *I think Leela needs some antibiotics. I want her to get over this illness soon.*

This parent is simply doing what he thinks is best for his child and he may argue vociferously for a specific treatment if he feels that she needs it. Again, antibiotics are of no use for a viral URI. But in this case, the practitioner needs to address two "patients"— the parent and the child. Educate both the parent and the child about the proper use of antibiotics.

→ We want Leela to get better soon as well. But after examining her closely, I find that there aren't any signs of a bacterial infection. I really think her symptoms are due to a viral infection, and these usually get better on their own in two to three days. I think antibiotics would just give her an upset tummy and diarrhea but do nothing for her cold. Instead, let us advise you about how to treat her symptoms. We will also see her back in the office at any time if she gets worse.

Perfect Phrases for Patients Requesting Medications with the Potential for Abuse

Mrs. Gordon is a 39-year-old woman with bipolar disorder and chronic back pain. She has recently started visiting your primary care office and has made requests for large amounts of narcotic pain medications at each office visit.

Healthcare providers can be placed in a quandary when patients ask for medications with the potential for abuse. It is our duty to help relieve pain in our patients, but we must do it in a safe and responsible way. Narcotics and benzodiazepines, two of the most commonly abused classes of medications, are powerful and can help relieve pain, but their misuse can lead to serious consequences, including death and disability.

Determining which patients have a genuine need for medications and which patients are "drug seekers" can be very challenging. Patients won't admit outright to "drug seeking" because they may be ashamed of their addiction or afraid that we won't write them prescriptions for the medications they desire. Nor are there any tests that can help us identify the patients who want medications for illicit use.

Some red flags for possible "drug-seeking" behavior are a prior history of drug or alcohol abuse, repeated requests for medication for the same complaint, multiple drug allergies, and requests for specific medications by name or milligram dose. But again, these red flags are not absolute indicators. Therefore, we have to rely on our clinical impression of the patient to determine whether they have a true medical need for a medication.

Bringing up the possibility of medication abuse with the patient in the above vignette can be awkward and difficult. The

Substance Abuse and Mental Health Services Administration advocates some general principles that may make this conversation easier.

■ Assure the patient that your motivation for the discussion is his or her overall health.

➔ I know this may be difficult to talk about, but I need to bring up your use of narcotic medications because I am concerned about your health.

■ Don't assume a judgmental or accusatory attitude, and assure the patient that you will maintain confidentiality.

➔ I'm not here to judge you, and the things we discuss will be kept confidential. I just want to make sure we do what is best for your health.

■ It is impossible to know exactly what our patients are going through, so try to empathize with them, whatever their situation may be.

➔ I've taken care of many patients with similar issues. I've seen firsthand how tough it can be.

■ Asking "open-ended" rather than "closed" questions can help avoid a pointed or confrontational interaction.

➔ [Closed] How long have you been abusing drugs?

➔ [Open] Do you think you have had some issues with drugs?

➔ [Closed] Why are you using so many pills?

➜ [Open] I've just told you about some of my concerns about your use of prescriptions. What do you think about what I've said?

➜ [Closed] Why should I keep writing you all these narcotic prescriptions?

➜ [Open] Are you concerned about your use of prescriptions?

It is impossible to know ahead of time exactly how a conversation about potential medication abuse will play out. Some patients may be open to a discussion and request help in dealing with their abuse issues, whereas others may become infuriated that you have even raised the subject. Keep these principles in mind, and don't judge your patients before you hear what they have to say.

➜ I do need to discuss something with you today. You have requested some very large doses of very strong narcotic pain medications. I know you have some issues with your back, but I'm concerned about your use of these medications and their effect on your health. Some patients, through no fault of their own, can get a little too reliant on these medications. Do you think you may have become dependent on narcotics?

➜ *I don't have any problems with pills. I need the oxycodone for my back. I'm allergic to ibuprofen, and acetaminophen just doesn't cut it.*

How far you want to go in discussing potential medication abuse with your patients is at your discretion. Nevertheless, if patients deny abusing medications but you still aren't comfortable giving them prescriptions, let them know why.

→ I appreciate your assurances about your use of these medications. Nevertheless, I'm not comfortable writing you a prescription for so many pills at one time. These are extremely powerful medications, and they can have serious and life-threatening side effects. I can write you a prescription for some non-narcotic pills. If that isn't satisfactory for you, I think it may be best if we refer you to a pain clinic—they may be able to do more for you.

Perfect Phrases for Parents Requesting Tests for Minors: Ethical Issues

Jean is a 16-year-old girl who is at her pediatrician's office for a checkup. Jean's mother pulls the pediatrician aside outside of the exam room and asks for her daughter to be tested for pregnancy and drugs.

→ *Jean has been acting funny lately. She also has been spending a lot of time with a boy from school. I'm worried she could be pregnant or doing drugs or drinking. Can you just do some tests to find out if she's pregnant or using drugs?*

The mother, as the guardian of this minor, can consent for tests on her daughter. Doing tests for pregnancy or drugs without the patient's knowledge, even if that patient is a minor, can raise some tough ethical and trust issues. Whether or not you, as a healthcare professional, order these tests depends on your own values and your relationship with the patient and the parent.

→ I don't think it's a good idea to do tests on your daughter without her knowledge. These tests aren't 100% accurate, either, so we won't be completely sure that your child is or isn't using drugs on the basis of one urine test or blood test.

If you don't feel it is a good idea to order the tests, make sure to offer alternatives to deal with the issues that the parent has raised.

→ Could we try something else to deal with your concerns? Would you like me to discuss the risks of drug abuse and teen pregnancy with your daughter? I can also give you a

Perfect Phrases for Patients Requesting Specific Treatments

Mr. O'Malley is a 56-year-old man with hypertension, who has come to his primary care doctor's office. He has had two weeks of low back pain that seems to be gradually improving with physical therapy.

→ *This back pain seems to be getting a little better but it's still bothering me. I really think I need an MRI (magnetic resonance imaging) of my body.*

Patients may want a certain test or medication for a specific reason. A friend or relative might have been diagnosed with a medical problem, and now they may be worried that they are suffering from the same condition as well. There may be no medical indication to order the test, but don't demean your patients or their reasoning behind the request for the test. Rather, try to find out why they want the test, and educate them about the options to address their concerns. Some patients may only be seeking reassurance about their symptoms, and discussing their symptoms can ease their concerns.

→ For back pain, we would limit the MRI to your lower back area. Is there any specific reason you want one? Are you worried about something in particular?

→ *I saw on TV that someone who had a slipped disc found out about it only after an MRI. What if I have the same problem?*

It is appropriate to make patients aware of the costs of the medications or tests they are requesting. The Centers for Medicare and

Medicaid Services estimates that almost 18% of the U.S. gross domestic product (GDP) was spent on healthcare in 2009. Any test, expensive or not, should be ordered only if a patient needs it.

→ An MRI can tell us about the discs in your back. But it is a very expensive test, and I'm not sure it would change what we are doing at present. You do seem to be improving with our current treatment plan. Let's stick with it. If your progress stalls or your condition worsens, I can order an MRI for you.

Mr. Massone is a 36-year-old man who is at a gastroenterologist's office for the first time to be evaluated for dyspepsia. The physician has examined him and is finishing up the encounter.

→ I think we should send you for testing for a stomach bacterium called *Helicobacter pylori*. We should also start you on a medicine called a proton-pump inhibitor, which should alleviate your symptoms.

→ *Umm, all right. Fine.*

If the patient's body language expresses discontent or the tone of voice indicates disagreement with your plan, don't ignore that cue. Rather, address this dissatisfaction right away. We must manage the expectations of our patients early in the development of our relationship with them.

→ You don't seem too happy with this plan. Is there anything you think we should be doing differently? What is the best way for me to help you today?

→ *Well, I came here because I thought I was going get a scope of my stomach. I can just go buy this medicine over the counter without even seeing you.*

→ I'll be happy to perform an examination of your stomach with a scope—that procedure is called an EGD (esophago-gastroduodenoscopy). But there are risks and costs associated with putting a camera into your stomach. I do think it's a good idea to rule out the common causes of a stomach upset before performing an invasive procedure such as an EGD. If the tests for *H. pylori* don't show anything and you get no relief from this medication, we will get you in for an EGD right away.

Mr. Larson is a 27-year-old man who is at the Emergency Department (ED) with a sore throat. The physician assistant is evaluating him.

→ *I have strep throat. I've had it a bunch of times. I just need to get my tonsils out today. Can you get me a throat surgeon?*

Patients can present to an outpatient office or an ED with expectations that medical problems can be fixed immediately. The patients may be fed up with their symptoms and can have unrealistic expectations. Let the patients know that you sympathize with their problems but that non-emergent medical conditions aren't operated on or addressed on an emergent basis. Make sure to end the encounter by providing the patient with some options for what can be done, not merely what cannot be done.

→ I'm sorry that you are experiencing a sore throat again. Unfortunately, we don't arrange for tonsillectomies through the ED. What I can do is examine you and prescribe antibiotics and pain medications if you need them. After that, I can refer you to a throat surgeon if you are still having problems.

CHAPTER 4

Perfect Phrases for Breaking Bad News to Patients and Their Families

Breaking bad news to patients or their loved ones can be a source of extreme stress for healthcare professionals. We are not always prepared for these difficult interactions in medical or nursing school. We might be concerned that our patients will not take the news well and that it could destroy all the hope they have. We can imagine that the patients or their loved ones will be angry with us. Finally, we may feel that we have failed in our job by not securing good outcomes for our patients.

How well these difficult conversations go depends on many factors. A pre-existing relationship between the healthcare provider and the patient can be comforting for all parties involved. Studies have shown that family members named the attitude of the doctor delivering the bad news, the doctor's ability to answer questions, and a private setting for the conversation as very important.

Unfortunately, it can be very hard to meet all of these goals for communication. Not all healthcare professionals know their patients very well. Some patients may be new to your practice, or they may have been just admitted to the hospital and you are meeting them for the first time. The fast pace of modern medicine does not always allow the time or place to sit down quietly and have long conversations. In addition, it is nearly impossible to anticipate how patients or their families will react to bad news.

In these instances, we have to do our best to deliver bad news professionally and with as much compassion as we can. Having a structure or "game plan" in place ahead of time can be beneficial.

Prepare to Give the News

- Try to arrange for a private and quiet place to have the discussion.
- Maintain a professional appearance—straighten your tie or white coat, check your hair in a mirror, and take off bloody clothing.
- Put your beeper or cell phone on vibrate.
- Ensure that you have a complete understanding of the prognosis or diagnosis you are about to present.
- Bring a social worker, chaplain, or nurse if you think it will help facilitate communication.

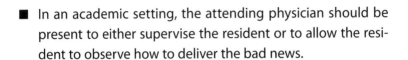

- In an academic setting, the attending physician should be present to either supervise the resident or to allow the resident to observe how to deliver the bad news.

Open the Discussion

- Clearly identify yourself, your role in the patient's care, and why you are there.

- Introduce yourself to everyone present and find out how they are related to the patient.

- Sit down at eye level.

Break the News

- Lead off with a very brief summary of the patient's clinical history.

- Give the patient or loved ones a warning statement—"I'm sorry but I have some bad news."

- Break the news using plain language—"The cancer has spread and has become much more serious" or "The car crash was very severe, and he died from his injuries."

- Pause to give the patient or loved ones time to absorb the information, grieve, or simply cry.

- Offer to answer any questions.

Close the Interaction

- Briefly let the patient or loved ones know what comes next— if the patient has cancer, it may mean seeing an oncologist; if the patient has died, it may mean the body will go to the medical examiner or the family will need to arrange for a funeral home to come collect the body.

■ If the patient has died, offer the family the chance to view the body, but let them know ahead of time if the patient has medical devices (intravenous tubes [IVs], endotracheal tubes) or traumatic injuries on the body.

■ Offer the patient and loved ones your continued support or Pastoral Care services.

■ Close with a final word of empathy.

This "game plan" won't work for every situation and every patient, so keep the following Pearls and Pitfalls in mind if you have to improvise.

Pearls

■ Look professional, and behave with the utmost professionalism. Families will remember this moment for the rest of their lives, and your appearance and demeanor will be part of that memory.

■ Gauge how much information the patient wants to know. Studies have shown that the vast majority of patients want full disclosure about their diseases, but some may not want to know specifics.

■ Some patients or loved ones appreciate physical touch. If you think it will be helpful, feel free to ask the patient, "Would like a hug or someone's hand to hold?"

■ Don't rush through the conversation. Allow people time to sit quietly, cry, or just process what you have told them.

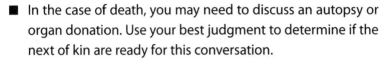

- In the case of death, you may need to discuss an autopsy or organ donation. Use your best judgment to determine if the next of kin are ready for this conversation.

- Highlight the positive things patients or loved ones have accomplished, such as "You've managed your disease so well since you were diagnosed" or "It sounds like you did just the right thing after your father collapsed."

Pitfalls

- Don't use medical terminology. Use plain, clear language, and speak slowly.

- Arrange for an interpreter if you do not speak the same language as that of the patient and family.

- If you don't know the answer to a question about what happened, don't guess; instead, let the family know that you will try to find out.

- Patients or loved ones may faint at hearing bad news. Make sure that everyone is sitting so that they don't fall and injure themselves.

- You may become the target for anger or blame over the bad outcome. Anticipate tough questions you may be asked.

- If a large number of people are present, find the one or two most closely related to the patient, and speak to them privately. Those people can then act as liaisons to the other people.

- If the interaction becomes overly heated or you anticipate violence, leave the room immediately.

- Always take someone else with you to the encounter, and always make sure you have a clear exit from the room.

Perfect Phrases for Breaking News of an Unfavorable Diagnosis

Mrs. Adams is a 52-year-old woman who visited her family physician's office two weeks ago to be evaluated for abdominal pain and weight loss. Her physician sent her for a computed tomography (CT) scan which showed extensive peritoneal carcinomatosis. She is back at the office to discuss the results of her scan.

When you are delivering a serious diagnosis, be honest but empathetic. Sit down at eye level with the patient.

➡️ Thanks for coming back in to discuss your test results. The CT scan results were sent over from the radiology center. I'm sorry to have to tell you this, but they are not good. It appears that you have a very serious cancer, and it has spread all over the inside of your abdomen. This must be just terrible news for you.

Sit quietly, and give the patient all the time you think she needs to absorb this devastating information. The patient or loved ones may have many questions, and you may not be able to answer all of them.

➡️ *Where did this cancer start? Is this going to kill me? How long do I have to live?*

Answer the questions to the best of your ability, but don't make up answers.

➡️ Those are all good questions, but I can't answer all of them. I want to arrange for you to see a cancer specialist as soon as possible.

Try to end the interaction on a positive note.

→ We both know that this is a very serious situation. At least we have found out why you have been in pain and losing weight. Now we can move forward and have you see the cancer doctor as soon as possible so we can try to deal with this. As your family doctor, I'll do my best to be there for you on the road ahead.

Mr. Smith is a 64-year-old man with a long smoking history who was diagnosed with lung cancer six months ago. Since then, he has been undergoing radiation therapy in an effort to shrink the tumors in his lungs. He is visiting his oncologist's office to discuss his recent positron emission tomography (PET) scan. Unfortunately, the PET scan shows that the lung cancer has widely metastasized.

Assessing what the patient or loved ones knows about the patient's condition is important. Some patients may be very knowledgeable about medical issues and very involved in their own care. In these cases, the patients may already be anticipating the bad news you are about to tell them because they are aware of the complications of their conditions. Other patients and families may be extremely naïve and have a very limited understanding of their diseases. Some families may even intentionally hide medical information from the patients because they fear how their loved ones will react to the information.

→ I know that you and your wife have been very involved in your care since your diagnosis of cancer. Just so that we are all on the same page, can you tell me what you know about the status of your cancer?

→ *Well, I know that it is in my lungs and that the radiation is supposed to be shrinking the tumors.*

→ Thank you. That is a good summary of what has happened so far. Do you understand why we did the PET scan last week?

→ *I guess it was to see if the cancer is getting smaller?*

→ That is one reason. The other is to see if the cancer has spread. Unfortunately, this imaging test shows that your cancer has spread outside of the lung. I want to make sure that you know how much more serious your condition is now that the cancer has spread.

→ *Oh no! This is what we were afraid of.*

It can be valuable to gauge how much the patient wants to know about his disease.

→ I know you didn't want to hear news like this. I wish things were different. As your disease has worsened, I feel that I should tell you some of the complications you may encounter. Would you like to discuss them?

→ *My wife and I have talked about this. We want to know every-thing about what is going on even if it's tough to take.*

→ OK. I'm going to respect your wishes, and I'll keep you informed about all aspects of your medical care.

Mrs. Jones is a 28-year-old woman who came to her gyne-cologist's office to be evaluated for pelvic pain and vaginal discharge. After examining the patient the gynecologist is concerned that the patient has a sexually transmitted infec-tion (STI).

Not all bad news that we give to patients is life- or limb-threatening. From a healthcare provider's point of view, most common STIs are relatively easy to treat and cure. Because STIs have less grave implications than more serious diagnoses such as ovarian cancer or a ruptured ectopic pregnancy, we may underestimate how difficult it may be for a patient to get this news.

Yet from the patient's point of view, an STI may be a horrifying diagnosis. It may be the first indication that a sexual partner has cheated on her, or the patient may be concerned that she will no longer be able to have children. In such instances, validate the patient's concerns and educate her about her disease.

→ I'm concerned that you may have an infection of your genital area that is sexually transmitted. I won't be 100% sure until the results of the samples I took from your vaginal area return from the lab, but I think it would be best to treat you for the STI even before the tests come back.

→ *Does this mean my boyfriend has been cheating on me?*

→ I can't say for sure. Your symptoms could be from a non–sexually transmitted infection, or it could be from dormant infection you got from a prior sexual partner. I can give your more answers once the tests come back. In the meantime, I would advise you to have all your sexual partners tested for STIs.

This same scenario can apply to other diagnoses that we make. For instance, a patient who fell and broke his wrist will probably recover fully from his injury in four to six weeks. Yet, if he is the sole breadwinner for his family, missing work for four to six weeks could be financially devastating. Try to keep the effect a diagnosis will have on a patient in mind when you disclose it to him.

Perfect Phrases for Breaking News of Death

According to the Centers for Disease Control and Prevention (CDC), more than 57% of Americans died in hospitals in 2007. Some of these deaths were due to chronic diseases and were expected, whereas others were sudden and unexpected. How the next of kin reacts to news of death can vary, depending on whether the news was expected or not.

Another factor affecting how the next of kin reacts is the healthcare provider's relationship with them. You may have a close relationship with a patient you have treated for many years. In contrast, in a hospital setting, you can be called upon to pronounce the death of an inpatient that you don't know anything about and have never met.

Mrs. Smith is a 79-year-old woman with a history of heart failure, who was brought in coding by the paramedics to your Emergency Department (ED). She was treated appropriately, but, unfortunately, she died. Her son has just arrived at the ED and is asking about her condition.

You have called Pastoral Care and asked for the son to be put into a quiet and private room. You have put on your physician's lab coat, checked your appearance in the mirror, and are on your way to speak to the son.

→ My name is Dr. Mason. I understand that you are Mrs. Smith's son?

Let the next of kin know your role in the patient's care.

➜ I am the doctor who has been in charge of your mother's care since she arrived.

Leading off with a very short summary of what has happened until the actual death of the patient can help ease families into the bad news.

➜ Your mother was brought here to the Emergency Department from her house about one hour ago. She was found lying in the kitchen. The paramedics did a great job of getting her here quickly and had already put a breathing tube in her throat because she was having trouble breathing. When she got here, her heart was not beating well. We gave her our very strongest medications and ended up having to do chest compressions to keep her blood circulating.

Giving the family a brief warning that you are about to give them bad news can give them a moment to brace for the news.

➜ I'm very sorry to have to tell you this . . .

The words "dead" or "died" might be considered harsh, but they are concrete words that are understood by all. Euphemisms such as "passed on" or "kicked the bucket" or "moved on to a better place" might be misinterpreted or considered insensitive by the patient's loved ones.

➜ . . . but your mother has died. We tried everything we could, but her heart never started beating on its own.

Pause, and give the loved one time to absorb this news. Allow them to cry or sit silently for as long as you think they need to.

When you do speak again, don't use phrases such as "it was his time" or "she is in a better place" that might seem disingenuous or judgmental. Instead, acknowledge that this is a sad situation.

➜ This must be very hard for you, and I can't imagine what you are going through.

Some people may be incredulous or simply cannot process the news and may be in denial. Express sympathy, but be upfront about the diagnosis or prognosis.

➜ *She can't be dead. I just talked to her yesterday! She must just be sleeping. Can't we just wake her up?*

➜ I'm very sorry. We did everything we could, but she did not come back.

The pain and suffering that a patient went through before death can be incredibly disturbing to that patient's loved ones. Loved ones may also feel guilty or responsible for the patient's death. If you don't believe that a patient suffered or that his or her death was no one's fault, some words of empathy can be invaluable. Don't say things about which you are unsure.

➜ She was unconscious the whole time, so I do not believe that she suffered. There was no way that you could have known that this was going to happen.

Offer crying people tissues and the services of the Pastoral Care office. In addition, people will often want to see the body of their loved one to say goodbye.

➜ Would you like to see her? Would you like us to arrange for a chaplain to visit with you?

The sight of invasive medical devices in the patient's body can disturb loved ones. Depending on the circumstances of death and the policies of your local medical examiner's office, the devices may need to stay in place if an autopsy is to be performed. Warn the patient's loved ones ahead of time that they should expect to see the devices.

➜ Before we take you to your mom, I have to let you know that she had a tube placed in her throat to help her breathe and she still has some tubes in her arms that we were delivering medicines through. These devices are still on her.

At some point, you are going to have to end the conversation and return to your other patients.

➜ Is there anything else I can do for you right now? I'm sorry to leave you, but I have to look in on some of my other patients. If you need anything else or have questions, please ask for me, and I will come back and speak to you some more.

Mr. Grover is an older man with many medical problems. He was recently admitted to the hospital for a serious case of pneumonia. His condition worsened during the night, and, unfortunately, he died. You are calling his son, who is his next of kin.

It is best to deliver bad news in person, but at times it may have to be done over the telephone. For instance, the next of kin may live far away from the hospital, or they may insist that you tell them the news over the phone.

→ Are you able to come to the hospital? Your father's condition has worsened, and we need you to come in.

→ *I live really far away from the hospital, and I have to work in the morning. Don't beat around the bush. Just tell me what's going on.*

Ask a few simple questions to gauge how informed the family is about the patient's condition.

→ Can you tell me what you know about your father's condition?

→ *The nursing home called me and said he was being taken to the hospital because he had a bad fever and cough. I know that he isn't too healthy overall to begin with.*

→ Yes, he was very ill when he got here to the hospital, and he was diagnosed with a bad case of pneumonia. Last night, he started to get worse. His oxygen levels began to drop, his breathing became labored, and his blood pressure fell. We gave him oxygen and eventually had to give him our very strongest medicines to help keep his blood pressure up. I am very sorry to have to tell you this, but his infection was too serious, and he has died.

→ *What? He's dead? Did you shock him? Dad had a bad heart. I've seen on TV people with bad hearts being shocked, and it always works. Did you get him a cardiologist? How come you let him die?*

Loved ones can react to bad news with anger and accusations. Don't take what they say personally or respond with anger. As a professional, you must always take the high road.

→ I promise you that we did all we could to try to save your father. I think his infection was too far along and it overwhelmed him.

→ *So it wasn't his heart?*

Answer loved ones' questions to the best of your ability, but don't conjecture or make up answers. If you don't know, you can say that you suspect something or that it is your opinion, but also tell them that you will do your best to find out and can get back to them.

→ I can't be 100 percent sure that he died from the infection, but it's my strongest medical opinion. We can't answer all the questions for sure without an autopsy.

Perfect Phrases for Breaking Bad News About Pediatric Patients

Unfavorable outcomes in the case of pediatric patients can be particularly stressful for all involved. The grief associated with a serious diagnosis or death of a child can devastate healthcare professionals and parents alike. When breaking news of a serious diagnosis, it is fitting to involve the child if he or she is at an appropriate age and level of maturity. Most children begin to understand the concept of death between ages six and nine years. As with patients of all ages, sit down at eye level, use simple words, and stop occasionally to make sure that everyone understands what you are conveying.

In situations where a child is critically ill and may die, it is important that a liaison be established between the family of the patient and the medical team. This liaison could be a nurse, medical student, or social worker, who can explain what is going on with the child and give the family regular updates. There is a growing trend toward bringing family members into the room when a child is being resuscitated. Studies have shown families appreciate being with their loved ones as they die, and it also gives the family the chance to see how hard everyone is working to save their loved one. If this type of family involvement is part of your practice, make sure that the liaison accompanies the family into the resuscitation area.

Justin is a 4-year-old boy who was found floating pulseless in his family's pool after being left unattended. He was admitted to the pediatric intensive care unit (PICU) after

being coded in the ED with return of spontaneous circulation. His clinical condition has further deteriorated and he is pulseless again. A social worker has gone out to the PICU waiting area to let his family know that Justin is being coded again.

Hopefully, by the time this child has been admitted to the PICU, his family knows how serious their child's condition is. If the family is to be present for the resuscitation, ensure that they have someone with them who can explain what is going on in layman's terms.

→ Justin's condition has taken a turn for the worse. The team is working on him right now. I can take you to his room if you would like to be there with him.

If the family is to be in the room, make sure that all of the staff knows that the family is there.

→ <u>Speaking to the staff in the room with the patient:</u> *Everyone please be aware that Justin's parents are going to be coming back and will be in the room as we work on Justin.*

→ <u>Speaking to Justin's parents:</u> *I'm sorry to have to tell you this, but Justin's condition has worsened, and his heart has stopped beating on its own. We are doing everything we can to get it started again. I'm going to ask you to stand over here to the side so that the team can work on him. Nurse Harriman will stand with you and explain what is going on.*

The family liaison should not use complex medical terms when speaking to the family. Don't say:

→ Justin coded, so we commenced ACLS (advanced cardiac life support) protocols and pushed pressors through a central line.

A family is more likely to understand and appreciate what is going on if the following is said:

→ That nurse is doing chest compressions to help the blood circulate to Justin's brain, and the doctor at the head of the bed is putting in a breathing tube so we can give Justin oxygen directly to his lungs.

If the child dies, the same principles used for breaking bad news about adult patients apply to cases involving pediatric patients as well. However, in the case of the death of a child, the reality of a life cut short does amplify the grief for everyone involved.

CHAPTER 5

Perfect Phrases for Dealing with Suspected Child Abuse, Elder Abuse, or Intimate Partner Violence

A s healthcare professionals, we have myriad duties that we must perform for our patients. One important duty, with both ethical and legal aspects, is to ensure that they live in a safe environment. Three populations of patients that are especially vulnerable to abuse are the young, the old, and those patients suffering from intimate partner violence (IPV).

Bringing up the possibility of abuse or violence with our patients can be a daunting task. We may be afraid that we will offend our patients and therefore lose their trust. The subjects we may have to broach can be taboo and may offend our own sensibilities just to think of them. We may not know the best way to bring up these subjects or even if we should involve the patient's family members. Having some key phrases and strategies ready may make these difficult conversations easier.

There are some common themes in abuse or violence among all three of these populations: dependence and fear. Until a certain age, all children are totally dependent on their parents or guardians for everything from shelter to food. The elderly can also be dependent on others, especially if age or disease has made them frail and they are not financially independent. An intimate partner may be dependent on his or her partner in many ways, including financially and emotionally.

The theme of dependence leads to the next theme, fear. Dependence may make people live through, and even accept, abuse or violence because of fear. They may fear that if they report the abuse, the perpetrators will kick them out of their homes, take away their children, stop loving them, and harm them more violently or even kill them. There is also the fear of shame in being identified as a victim of abuse.

The dependence and fear associated with abuse can be significantly negative influences that alter a patient's behavior and even their health. We may not be able to prove or verify any of our suspicions about abuse or violence, but thankfully, that is not our job. Rather, the most important thing we can do as healthcare professionals is to consider the possibility that our patients are or have been victims of abuse or violence. We can then report the suspected abuse or offer further resources to a patient or the family.

Keep the following points in mind when dealing with suspected abuse.

Abuse Takes on Many Forms

- It is easy to diagnose abuse in a patient with the chief complaint "My boyfriend hit me" or a small child with multiple long bone fractures.
- However, abuse can be in the form of physical or sexual violence, neglect, and emotional abuse.
- The emotional and physical trauma from abuse may manifest in different ways in different patients.
- Patients with repeat visits to the clinic or the Emergency Department (ED) for non-specific somatic complaints may actually be suffering from abuse.
- Include all forms of abuse in your differential diagnosis when evaluating patients.

Abusers Come in All Shapes and Sizes

There are certain characteristics that may be found in people who abuse others:

- A history of suffering abuse themselves
- Drug- or alcohol-related disorders
- Personality disorders and psychiatric problems
- Lower socioeconomic status

These characteristics are not present in all cases, and an abuser may or may not have them.

Abuse is found across the entire racial, ethnic, and socioeconomic spectrum.

Perform a Thorough History and Physical Exam

- When the history of the injury or illness cannot explain the clinical findings, consider abuse.

- A complete history and physical exam is vital if you suspect abuse of any form.
- Ensure that your physical exam is standardized and well documented, as it may become legal evidence.
- Transfer patients who may need a specialized exam or interview to an appropriate facility.
- Pay attention to any family members or loved ones with the patient. Do they seem overly aggressive toward staff or overly protective of the patient? Does the patient seem to fear them?

Acknowledge and Respect Cultural Differences

- Understand that in other cultures or countries, certain behaviors or customs may not be considered abuse.
- Understand that immigrants or minorities may hesitate to contact law enforcement because they may fear deportation or unfair treatment.
- Ensure the patients and family that a language interpreter, in person or by phone, is available.

Documentation Is Important

- Document what a patient or family member says as direct quotes.
- Activate other resources, such as a social worker or the child protective services (CPS), early, and document their input.
- Remember that what you document may be used in a court of law to protect your patient or to prosecute an abuser.

Perfect Phrases for Suspected Child Abuse

According to the U.S. Department of Health and Human Services, in 2009, there were more than 2.5 million reported cases of suspected cases of child abuse. This statistic only reflects reported cases of suspected abuse, so it is quite possible that the actual number of instances is much higher.

Healthcare professionals are mandated reporters, meaning that we are legally obligated to report all cases of suspected child abuse to the appropriate authorities. In other words, to make a report, we don't have to be absolutely positive that child abuse has occurred; we only need to suspect it.

A woman brings Carter, her 8-month-old son, to the ED. She tells the triage nurse that the child has not been moving his right leg for the past day. On exam, the child's right thigh is bruised and swollen, and he cries when it is palpated. An x-ray of the extremity shows a spiral fracture of the femur.

Children suffer all types of musculoskeletal injuries due to accidents, such as falls while playing. Certain types of injuries and fractures rarely occur in children who fall while playing or in children who are below one year of age and, thus, not old enough to walk or run on their own.

Injuries Suspicious for Abuse

- Patterns—injuries that outline an object, such as a hand, teeth, or an electrical cord
- Bruising at areas away from bony prominences (examples of prominences are the shin or forehead)
- Multiple bruises at various stages of healing

Fractures Suspicious for Abuse

- ■ Long bone fracture in a patient who hasn't started walking
- ■ Metaphyseal fractures
- ■ Fractures of the rib, scapula, spinous process, or skull

→ Carter's x-ray looks like he has broken his femur—that's the bone in the thigh area. It's unusual for a child of his age to break this bone. Do you know how this might have happened?

→ *I'm not sure. When I picked him up from his crib last night, he cried a lot. This morning, when I was changing him, he was still crying. His leg looked swollen, and he wasn't moving it.*

→ Did Carter have any falls or accidents recently?

A long bone fracture, in this case, should not occur in a child who cannot walk by himself. We should try to obtain a history that can explain the injury that we have diagnosed. This case must be reported to the CPS due to the nature of the injury. Even with less severe injuries, if you cannot obtain a history that can reasonably explain the injury or that has inconsistencies, you should suspect abuse.

→ *Nothing happened to him. He was fine until last night.*

When questioning parents or guardians, don't assume an accusatory tone, even when you are highly concerned about possible abuse. It is unlikely that you will know all of the facts when you evaluate the child. The parent or guardian with the child may not be the one who actually injured the child, or they may not even be aware that someone else may have abused their child. Moreover, once a parent or guardian feels that he or she is being accused of something, they can become angry and defensive.

From that point onward, they may be less likely to cooperate with any evaluation of the child.

→ This kind of injury can occur when someone is rough with a child. Do you know anyone that might have handled Carter in a rough way?

→ *No. I dropped him off of the couch last week by accident, but it was onto a carpet, and the drop was less than two feet. I didn't do anything to hurt him! How dare you accuse me of hurting him!*

Even if you have maintained a non-accusatory tone, parents or guardians may take offense with your questions. Try to focus the inquiry on securing what is best for the health of the child. A social worker, if one is available, may be able to help moderate tense situations and redirect the anger of parents.

→ I'm not accusing you or anyone else of hurting Carter on purpose. But this is a pretty serious fracture, and we need to figure out how this happened. I know you want to figure this out, too.

The parent of this child is not offering any information that can reasonably explain this injury. This child needs to be admitted to the hospital to be evaluated by an orthopedic surgeon and also by CPS. Let the parent know your plan and that you will need to contact CPS.

→ We need to admit Carter to the hospital to see the bone doctors. I am also required by the state to get in touch with children's services when a child has this kind of injury. They will help us check out every possible way that Carter could have been injured so that it doesn't occur again.

It is not clear that you will be discharging the child to a safe environment. Regardless of the parent's wishes, this child should not go home. In less clear-cut cases, you could hold onto the child in the ED or clinic until the CPS can evaluate him.

A young couple brings their 2-month-old son Timmy to the ED. They tell the physician that the child "has not been acting right" for the past couple of hours. On exam, the child is less than 5 percent of his expected weight on a growth chart and is lethargic but afebrile. He has faint bruises in the shape of hands, wrapping from front to back on both sides of his chest.

Children must be completely undressed, including having their diapers removed, and examined from head to toe. They should have their height and weight measured and the measurements compared with standardized growth charts. These steps are even more vital in children who cannot yet speak, as they cannot tell you what has happened to them or if they are in pain from an injury.

→ <u>After completely undressing and thoroughly examining the child:</u> I'm a little concerned about Timmy. He has some bruising on him, and I'm worried that his behavior isn't normal. Did anything unusual happen at home?

→ *Nothing happened. He was crying, and so I went to check up on him. I fed him and put him back to bed.*

→ *I haven't seen him since this morning. When I got home from work, he wasn't acting right, so we brought him right here.*

The findings of bruising on the thorax and a depressed mental status suggest that this child may have suffered a central nervous system (CNS) injury due to abuse. A child this young will need further testing to make sure that his presentation is not due to other processes, such as an infection or a metabolic derangement. He will also need a specialized exam, imaging, and monitoring for the possibility of a brain injury. If your facility does not have the resources for these tests, this child should be transferred to a facility where these tests can be performed.

→   I think it would be best for Timmy if we watch him in the hospital. His behavior change could be due to many different things, and I'm not sure which one it is yet. We will need to do some tests on him and monitor his health.

Tell the parents what you are going to do and why, but avoid taking an accusatory tone. Referring to the CPS as "child services" is one way to keep the tone of the conversation generic until you know more facts. Always emphasize that what you are doing is in the best interest of the patient.

→   I also want to let you know ahead of time that I have to report this case to child services. You should expect some people from this agency to get in touch with you, and they may even come to your house. Sometimes, they can give you advice on "child-proofing" your house.

In cases that are less clear cut, it is still prudent to get help early in the care of the patient by calling CPS. They may arrange for the child to stay with a close family member or even come out to your facility to initiate an investigation. In these situations, the worst-case scenario is not a parent being angry with you because you have "accused" them of abuse—it is discharging a patient to be injured or die in an unsafe environment.

A woman brings her 9-year-old daughter to the pediatrician's office because she thinks her boyfriend has been "touching" her daughter inappropriately. The mother had called the police, who told her to take her daughter to the doctor's office.

In this case, the patient has presented with abuse already suspected. Unfortunately, it can be very challenging to interview young children about possible abuse because their understanding of right and wrong is limited. They may feel pressured to please their interviewer by offering certain answers. Some social workers, clinical psychologists, and pediatricians are specially trained and have expertise in carrying out forensic interviews with children. In cases where there is concern about sexual abuse, the child should be transferred to a facility that has expertise in examining children for sexual abuse.

When interviewing a pediatric patient about possible abuse, make sure to ask simple, open-ended, non-leading questions rather than closed or leading questions. Document everything that is said word for word and in quotes. Try to limit questions that require yes or no answers, as children may answer in the affirmative in an attempt to please the interviewer. Finally, use words that are age appropriate to the patient. A young child may not know what the word "vagina" means, so you may need to refer to their genital area as "private parts."

Open Questions

- Did someone hurt you?
- How did they touch you?
- Where on your body were you touched?
- Who touched you?
- Tell me more about what happened.

Closed Questions

- Did your mother's boyfriend molest you?
- What did he do when he molested you?
- Was he touching your private areas?
- When did he molest you?

Attempt to interview the parents and the child separately. Some parents may resist allowing you to speak to the child alone. This resistance can be motivated by a fear of exposing something that has been perpetrated against the child. It can also be borne out of an overprotective parental drive for the child. A parent's resistance to leave the child alone with you should contribute to your overall clinical suspicion of the situation, but it should not stand as proof of abuse on its own.

→ <u>To the parent:</u> Could you please step out of the room for just a few minutes?

→ *Why do I need to leave? I want to know what you are going to ask my daughter.*

→ I speak to all of my patients in private. This is standard practice at this hospital.

Unfortunately, a benign interview and a normal physical exam do not rule out physical or sexual abuse. The overall clinical suspicion must be based on speaking with the patient, his or her parents or guardians, and a physical exam. In cases where you are concerned that a child could be in danger, err on the side of caution and get help.

Perfect Phrases for Suspected Elder Abuse

The population of the United States is rapidly aging. The U.S. Census Bureau estimates that by 2020, there will be almost 55 million citizens, or 16.3 percent of the total population, over the age of 65 years. As some in this graying population develop dementia or physical infirmities, they become dependent on others to care for them. This dependence puts them at risk for abuse of all kinds: physical, sexual, emotional, neglect, and financial or material exploitation.

Identifying older patients who are victims of abuse can be challenging. Older patients may have severe dementia or medical problems that render them unable to communicate. In this case, they, like children, cannot verbalize if they are in pain or if someone has been abusing them. They may also be afraid that they will be forced out of their nursing home or their family's house if they disclose abuse.

Nevertheless, healthcare professionals are mandated reporters of elder abuse, and we must be vigilant to include abuse in our differential diagnoses when evaluating older patients. As with all patients, a careful head-to-toe physical exam is vital to ensure that no injuries or findings are missed.

Mrs. Mathew is an 86-year-old woman who lives at home with her daughter. She has multiple medical problems, including severe dementia, and is bed bound. Her son who is visiting from out of town has brought his mother to the ED to be evaluated for the "redness" on her back. The patient's mental status makes her incapable of answering any of your questions coherently. On exam you find a thin

woman wearing a soiled diaper who has severe decubitus ulcers.

The daughter has not been adequately caring for this patient, who is most likely a victim of neglect. However, many cases of elder abuse may have much less dramatic presentations. In situations where the possibility of abuse is less clear-cut, we will have to use all our clinical skills to explore our suspicions of abuse.

Be sure to question a patient and his or her suspected abusers separately. Carry out these conversations in a non-threatening and non-judgmental manner. In the acute setting, it is unlikely that you can even be sure that the person you are interviewing is the actual abuser. The goal is not to act as proxies for law enforcement but to stop the abuse and keep our patients safe.

Closed and Aggressive Questions

- Your mother looks awful. Why haven't you been taking care of her?
- How could you let her get like this?
- Your mother could only get ulcers like this if she was being abused.
- Was it you abusing her, or was it your sister?

Open and Explorative Questions

- I'm concerned about your mother's medical condition. Is it stressful to care for her at home?
- Can you tell me about her care at home?
- Have you noticed any changes in your mother's overall condition recently?

- Have your siblings been helping with your mother's care?
- Does anyone else help care for her?

Older patients can suffer from paranoia or delusions due to dementia, which limits their ability to answer questions accurately. In these cases, you will have to rely on your physical exam, prior records on this patient, and discussion with family or caregivers. The following are some physical exam findings that are suggestive of abuse in older patients.

- Poor general hygiene
- Lying in urine or feces
- Pressure ulcers
- Fractures that don't make sense in a patient with limited ambulation
- Bruising in patterns suggesting restraints or beatings with objects (extension cords)
- Sedated patients who may have been intentionally overmedicated

This patient must be admitted to the hospital for wound care, and the appropriate authorities must be contacted. In some cases, patients may not have injuries that necessitate admission to a hospital. If they are not going to be discharged to a safe environment, you must admit them or arrange for them to go to a safe place, such as a different family member's house.

Mrs. Christopher is a 77-year-old woman who has numerous medical problems and lives in a nursing home. She was brought to her family doctor's office for evaluation of

a fever. As the doctor is examining her, the patient says, "They've been mean to me at the nursing home."

Elder abuse takes on many forms. It is incumbent on us, as healthcare providers, to explore if this patient is suffering from abuse when she says someone has been "mean" to her. Ask open-ended questions, using simple language. If a patient doesn't describe a specific complaint, it is important to ask about all forms of abuse.

General Safety

- Do you feel safe at your house (or nursing home)?
- Are you afraid of anyone?
- Are you being well cared for?

Physical Abuse

- Has anyone at your house hit you?
- Have you been tied down or locked in your room?

Sexual Abuse

- Has anyone ever done anything sexually to you against your wishes?

Financial Abuse

- Do you control your own finances/checkbook?
- Have you signed financial papers that you didn't understand, such as a will or bank forms?

- Do you rely on others for your housing, or do others rely on you for money?

Neglect

- Does someone help you bathe, eat, and get your medications?
- Are you left alone often?
- Are you hungry or thirsty at home?
- Does someone help you get your walker or hearing aids?
- If you need help, does someone come to help you?

Emotional Abuse

- Do you feel lonely?
- Do you have a lot of arguments with the people you live with?
- Do people at home yell at you or call you names?

Older patients may have physical infirmities but still have sharp, clear minds. Give them a chance to answer your questions, and be sure to thoroughly explore any areas of possible abuse. You should take patients' dementia and other medical comorbidities into account when interviewing them. Do not ignore their complaints of abuse simply because of their mental status.

Perfect Phrases for Suspected Sexual Violence and Intimate Partner Violence

Sexual violence (SV) is sexual activity that occurs without consent and includes stalking, peeping, harassment, threats, and physical contact ranging from unwanted touching to rape. According to the Centers for Disease Control and Prevention (CDC), almost 11 percent of women and just over 2 percent of men report being victims of SV at some point in their life. These numbers could actually be much higher because it is estimated that only one in three instances of SV are reported.

Intimate partner violence (IPV) is similar to SV, but it occurs between two people who have a close relationship. IPV can include physical violence, sexual violence, threats of violence, and emotional abuse. The CDC estimates that every year 4.8 million women experience IPV-related assaults and rapes and at least 1,600 women die from IPV. In addition, the Bureau of Justice reports that among all violent crimes committed against women, fully 20 percent were IPV related.

These and other statistics clearly show that SV and IPV are highly prevalent in the United States and that the vast majority of this violence is directed toward women by men. There are a number of factors that place people at risk for being victims of SV or IPV:

- Female gender
- Pregnancy
- Age less than 35 years
- Growing up in a family with domestic violence
- Previous victim of SV or IPV

- Physical or mental disability
- Drug or alcohol abuse
- Low socioeconomic status

Victims of SV and IPV can present to a healthcare professional for almost any reason. They may come for medical treatment of physical injuries suffered during an assault or for treatment of sexually transmitted infections (STIs). In addition, people who are or have been victims of SV or IPV can suffer from psychological injuries that may manifest as depression, mood changes, or even vague somatic complaints. Unlike in the case of abuse of children or the elderly, healthcare professionals are not mandated to report SV and IPV. Therefore, the help that we can offer these victims is limited by how much help they are willing to accept.

Mrs. Lau is a 26-year-old woman who has had repeated visits to her family doctor for abdominal pain. She has had blood tests and a pelvic ultrasound that were all normal. During these office visits, her affect has been flat, and her mood seems depressed.

You should include IPV in your differential diagnoses when evaluating patients. Although IPV may seem like an uncomfortable topic to discuss with your patients, it should be a part of standard history taking and physical exam. Asking about IPV with standardized screening questions can make it a more routine inquiry and therefore a less uncomfortable topic.

A helpful mnemonic for IPV screening, originally developed by the Massachusetts Medical Society, is **RADAR**.

■ **R**outinely ask your patients about IPV. Do this in private.

→ Mrs. Lau, thanks for coming in today to follow up on your abdominal pain. I have a few other questions that I ask all my patients.

■ **A**sk directly about IPV. Maintain a non-judgmental and caring attitude. The following are examples of open-ended questions that can open a discussion about IPV.

Do you feel safe at home?

Did someone hurt you?

Did someone do something to you that you didn't want done?

How did this person hurt you?

Where on your body were you hurt?

Is there anyone at home that is hurting you?

Do you feel safe in your current relationship?

How do you feel about your home life?

Are you afraid of your partner or anyone else?

■ **D**ocument what your patient has told you. Note any injuries you have observed, and write down the patient's statements in quotes. What you document may later become a vital part of a patient's legal record. If the patient denies IPV, make sure to document that you asked about it.

→ *The patient states "Things are not great at home right now" but won't say whether or not she feels safe and denies violence.*

■ **A**ssess your patient's safety and willingness to get help. Is the patient safe at home? Are her children safe? Is the patient willing to get help at this time?

→ Mrs. Lau, some things you told me today make me a little concerned about your home situation. Are you sure that you feel safe at home? Would you like to talk about this now?

■ **R**espond, and review the options with your patient. Acknowledge what the patient has told you, and let her know what her options are for further help.

Thanks for sharing with me today; I know this must be difficult to talk about.

Would you like to talk about what is happening at home?

Would you like some help?

Would you like to know about some resources for getting help?

A patient may not disclose IPV until asked about it on multiple occasions at multiple visits. That is exactly why it is important to routinely screen your patients for IPV. Your patient may not be a victim of IPV, and he or she will never have anything to disclose. If you don't think of it and don't ask about it, you will never diagnose it.

Ms. Wimberly is a 19-year-old woman who has presented to an outpatient clinic with pain in her shoulder. She is evaluated by a physician and is noted to have pain in her shoulder with range of motion and bruising on her upper arm. Her boyfriend has accompanied her to the clinic.

As in pediatrics, certain physical exam findings, such as bruising, especially around the head and face, should raise suspicion of IPV. This is even more true if the injuries are not explained by the history of the present illness.

→ The nurse told me that you are having some shoulder pain. What happened to your shoulder?

→ *She slipped on the sidewalk. I just need her to get an x-ray to make sure nothing is broken.*

The intimate partners of some patients can be overly controlling in medical settings. This behavior doesn't rule IPV in or out, but it should further raise your suspicion.

→ I'll be happy to order an x-ray. Before I do that I need to examine the patient. <u>To the patient's boyfriend:</u> Can you please step out while I examine the patient?

→ *Why do I need to leave? Can't you just order the x-ray?*

All patients should have at least some portion of their interview or physical exam in private so that they may ask about concerns that they wish to be kept confidential from even their loved ones.

→ I speak to all of my patients in private. It's routine and something that all the doctors in this ED do.

Ask open-ended, non-leading questions.

→ <u>To the patient in private:</u> I've noticed that some of your injuries seem like they might have come from someone being rough with you. Has anyone been rough with you?

It is very important to make sure that the patient does not feel that you will blame her for what has happened to her. She may already feel ashamed or embarrassed about what has happened to her. Make sure she knows that you can be trusted to keep what she tells you confidential.

→ Nobody deserves to be hurt by someone else. Anything you tell me will be confidential, and I won't do anything about what you tell me unless you want me to.

The patient may not be ready or willing to tell you about IPV. Make sure the patient knows that you are always available to help if needed.

→ It is completely up to you if you want to get some help. But if you change your mind we are always here. Let me give you the phone numbers of some people who can help and also the name of our social worker here at the hospital.

Offer patients literature on IPV or the services of a social worker so that they can have somewhere to turn to if they choose to get help in the future.

Ms. Desai is a 21-year-old woman who was brought to the ED by the police. She went to the police after being sexually assaulted at a fraternity party. The police are requesting that the victim have a medical examination and that evidence be collected.

Victims of SV have undergone a terrible experience. They should be shown compassion and treated with respect. It may be your job as a healthcare professional to collect physical evidence (by using a "rape kit") from the patient's body that may be used against her attackers. Keep the following points in mind when examining a victim of SV.

■ Put the patient in a private room.

→ I can't even imagine what you have gone through. We are going to do everything that needs to be done to help you.

■ Get help from a Sexual Assault Nurse Examiner (SANE) or social worker, if available.

→ I'm going to bring Nurse Catherine in with us. She is a nurse who specializes in helping people who have been assaulted.

■ Provide a brief overview of the interview and the examination process.

→ First, we are going to ask you some questions, and then we will perform a physical exam. After that, we will answer any questions you have and offer you any treatments or medicines you may need.

■ Explain that you will have to ask sensitive and perhaps painful questions.

→ We do have to ask you some very personal and painful questions about what happened. I know it will be hard to answer some of these questions, but we are asking them so that we can take care of you to the best of our abilities.

■ Explain that you will have to perform a detailed physical exam to collect evidence.

→ We need to perform a physical exam and collect samples from your body. Parts of the physical exam will involve your genital area. I know this will be uncomfortable for you, but it's important to perform these tests because they can be used as evidence against whoever did this to you.

- Offer prophylaxis for pregnancy, STIs, and human immunodeficiency virus (HIV) and resources for follow-up.

→ We are going to give you medications to prevent several common sexually transmitted infections. We will also put you in touch with people who can help you as you go forward.

For More Information

For detailed guidelines on diagnosing and reporting child abuse in your state refer to the website of the Child Welfare Information Gateway: www.childwelfare.gov. The American Academy of Pediatrics also has a detailed website with information on child abuse and neglect: www.aap.org/sections/scan.

The National Center on Elder Abuse, a part of the U.S. Administration on Aging, is an excellent resource for more information on elder abuse. Visit their website at: www.ncea.aoa.gov.

The CDC website has diagnostic and treatment information for healthcare professionals caring for victims of SV and IPV: www.cdc.gov/ViolencePrevention/sexualviolence. To find resources for victims of SV or IPV see the website of the Rape, Abuse & Incest National Network: www.rainn.org.

CHAPTER 6

Perfect Phrases for Dealing with Difficult Colleagues

There is an inherent hierarchical power structure in most clinical settings. At the top of this hierarchy is the attending physician. His or her orders for the patient's care are carried out by nurses and allied healthcare workers. In an academic setting, there are other layers of physicians below the attending physician, such as fellows and residents, who also write orders and perform procedures.

This power structure has many beneficial aspects, as more senior practitioners supervise the actions of physicians still in training. However, this structure can lead to abuses of power and "talking down" to people lower in the hierarchy. In addition, as in any organization, there can be significant conflict among people within the same level of hierarchy.

Excellent patient care can be provided only with good communication among the patient's providers. Therefore, the interactions among healthcare professionals are as important as the interactions between healthcare providers and their patients and families. In fact, the Joint Commission, which accredits and certifies more than 18,000 healthcare organizations and programs in the United States, has a standard that specifically supports a constructive and positive relationship among healthcare professionals in the interests of quality patient care and safety.

When conflicts do arise among colleagues, within and between different "levels" of the hierarchy, it is best to address the conflicts as soon as possible. Always try to speak directly to the involved party first. Although at times unpleasant, direct communication is typically the best method to resolve disagreements and misunderstandings. It is important to try to resolve problems on your own first. If the issue is not satisfactorily resolved, you may need to bump up the issue to a higher authority, such as a nurse manager or a department chair.

It is never acceptable to play out conflicts in front of patients. As healthcare professionals, we should behave impeccably around all patients. Even if you lose your temper and the conflict is going to descend into name calling or yelling, do it in private and out of patients' earshot. Squabbling in front of patients does not make us look smart, competent, or caring but rather childish and unprofessional.

Finally, if you think anything was said or done that was harassing or offensive to gender, race, religious views, or sexual orientation, document exactly what happened and when and

Perfect Phrases for Conflicts Among Healthcare Professionals at the Same Level

There can be disagreements among colleagues at the same hierarchical level—physician-to-physician, resident-to-resident, or nurse-to-nurse. It is best to resolve these conflicts at the personal level. In some instances, when a disagreement cannot be settled between two people, the dispute might need to be "bumped up the chain" to a department chair or a nurse manager.

An attending surgeon is concerned that an admitted patient may have an esophageal perforation. He has requested that the department of radiology perform a contrast swallow study. The attending radiologist is hesitant to perform the contrast swallow study and would rather perform a chest computed tomography (CT) scan. The surgeon has called the radiologist on the phone.

→ From what you are telling me, I don't think this patient has an esophageal perforation. Let's just get a CT scan of the chest instead.

In instances like this, it is easy to get in a "defensive mode" because another healthcare professional has questioned your medical decision making.

→ I just examined this patient, and you don't know what you are talking about. Just get me the contrast swallow!

Instead of reacting to the radiologist's suggestions as an attack, try more constructive ways to address this conflict.

→ I appreciate your input, but I have to admit that I don't understand why you would suggest a CT rather than a contrast swallow. Can you tell me how it would be more beneficial to the patient?

Acknowledging the other person's suggestions and expressing appreciation for his or her opinion can help calm emotions all around. Later, state your side of the issue clearly and politely.

→ I hear your point about the CT scan, and I appreciate your input. At this point, my biggest concern for this patient is an esophageal perforation. A perforation would be a life-threatening diagnosis for this patient, so I need to exclude this diagnosis as soon as possible. I think the contrast swallow is the test I need.

A common impediment to cordial communication between healthcare professionals is that many interactions take place over the phone. When two people are standing in front of each other, rather than just speaking on the phone, it is much harder for either party to be belligerent. If possible, consider going to meet your colleague in person somewhere in the hospital to resolve the conflict in person.

An attending emergency physician (EP) has evaluated a patient with chest pain and feels that the patient should be admitted to the hospital for further testing and observation. She has called the inpatient physician (IP) to admit the patient. The IP does not think the patient needs to be admitted and also wants a cardiology consultant to see the patient before the IP will evaluate her.

Conflicts over whether or not patients should be admitted to the hospital are common. With the ballooning cost of healthcare in America and the increased emphasis on managing patients on an outpatient basis, it is important to admit only those patients who need admission. However, saving money should not be the priority; our decisions should always be guided by what we think is best for our patients.

→ I just looked over this patient's labs on the computer, and I'm not convinced that she needs to be admitted. Before I consider admitting this patient, I'll need you to call Dr. Marhefka of cardiology to come evaluate her in the Emergency Department (ED).

Often, a physician may ask a patient to see a consultant. Keep in mind that a consultation from a physician is a resource. The patient will be billed for the evaluation, and the consultant's time will have been used to see that patient when his or her knowledge or skills may have been better served by treating another patient.

Before you disagree outright with a colleague's request, make sure that you understand the reasoning behind the request. Also, make sure that you clearly explain your own thinking. Conflicts can often stem from misunderstandings; simple clarification of the reasoning on both sides can help clear up conflicts.

→ There are some aspects of this patient's history and physical exam that I find concerning, and I think the patient would benefit from admission for some more testing. Please tell me what your thoughts are. Also, I can speak to the cardiology department about this patient, but can you tell me why you think this patient would benefit from see-ing a cardiologist?

If a patient is not admitted and you feel that he or she should have been, make sure you carefully document, in direct quotes, your reasoning and any conversations you had with consultants. If the patient suffers a bad outcome, you should have documen-tation of your goals for that patient's care. Continued conflict may require resorting to written hospital policies or the use of higher authorities to resolve the conflict for the patient's benefit.

Nurse Radis is coming on shift and will be taking the sign-out from Nurse Leist. Nurse Radis notices that a large num-ber of patient care tasks have been signed out to him. These tasks should normally be performed before the patients are signed out.

The nurse coming on shift could easily be annoyed by the extra work he has ahead of him.

→ I can't believe that you left me with all this work to do. These tasks clearly should have been done during your shift. I'm going to have a word with our supervisor about you!

Before jumping to conclusions or expressing anger, ascertain why these tasks weren't done. There may have been circum-stances beyond Nurse Leist's control that could have affected her work.

→ I'm curious because there seems to be a lot of work from your shift that I will need to do. Was there a problem get-ting them done today?

➜ We had a very sick admission, and two of my patients coded during the shift. My time and energy were focused on those patients, and there was no way that I could get to the other tasks. I'm sorry that they have to be signed out to you. Would you like me to stay a bit longer to help you out?

➜ OK, I understand. We've all had busy days like that. Thanks for offering to stay, but I can take it from here.

Nurse Leist may have a less reasonable explanation for the amount of work being signed out. It still does not serve anyone well to get angry. Nurse Radis can express that he doesn't appreciate getting work that should have already been completed and offer a solution to the problem.

➜ I don't know, I guess that I just didn't get to those things.

➜ Since this was work that should have been completed before sign-out, perhaps you should stay a bit to help get them done. In the future, you should ask for a nurse aide to come help you when you get overwhelmed by patient care duties. On really busy days, I've asked Diane, the nurse manager, to come down to the floor and help out for a few hours.

Perfect Phrases for Conflicts Among Healthcare Professionals at Different Levels

A 56-year-old man presents to the ED with chest pain. His electrocardiogram (ECG) shows evidence of an acute myocardial infarction, and the patient is hypotensive. The attending physician tells the resident physician to administer nitroglycerin. The resident is very concerned that administering nitroglycerin may dangerously lower the patient's blood pressure.

The relationship between the attending (supervising) physician and the resident physician (who is in training) is essentially that of a boss and an employee. The attending physician is more experienced and has the ultimate responsibility of ensuring both optimal patient care and optimal education of the resident. The resident has much less experience and relies upon the guidance of the attending physician. This relationship should be a nurturing one, but conflict can arise in multiple areas. The resident may be concerned that voicing an opinion that contradicts the attending physician's decision may result in a negative evaluation.

Ideally, the clinical environment should be one where every member of the healthcare team feels free to speak up on issues of patient safety. In the real world, the inherent power differentials in the field of medicine can make people lower on the chain of command feel too intimidated to speak up. The resident has a valid concern about this patient's safety and should find a way to bring up his concerns.

→ Are you kidding? Nitroglycerin will drop the blood pressure even more and probably kill the patient! I'm not giving nitro, and I'm not going to take care of this patient anymore.

There may be a good reason for the treatment advice or a reason that the resident may not know about. However, there are better ways to bring up his concerns.

→ I recently read that nitroglycerin can drop a patient's blood pressure and that it should not be given with low blood pressure. You seem sure that we should give this medication. For my own education, can you explain to me why we should give nitro in this situation?

→ I'm a little reluctant to order nitroglycerin because I haven't seen it used when a patient's blood pressure is this low. Are you sure this drug is safe in this situation?

An attending surgeon and a resident are performing a colonoscopy on an older man with suspected colon cancer. The resident is having trouble holding the colonoscope steady while the surgeon performs a biopsy.

The difference in knowledge and experience between an attending physician and a resident can manifest itself in the way residents develop treatment plans or perform procedures. Some attending physicians may become impatient with the performance of residents and can raise their voices or become verbally abusive.

→ What the hell is wrong with you? Is this the first time you've held a scope? Hold the scope steady so I can get this biopsy!

No one in medicine, regardless of his or her performance, deserves verbal abuse. It is probably not worthwhile for a resident to confront a supervising physician over a single episode of abusive language. However, a pattern of abusive or derogatory language should be discussed initially with the attending physician in question. The resident should try to discuss the physician's hostile comments in a respectful manner and in private. Pick one of the following comments as a way to open a conversation.

→ I'd like to ask you not to raise your voice when talking to me. If you have any negative feedback about my performance, please let me know specifically how you feel that I might improve.

→ I would like to become a better physician and improve my performance. Yelling at me and making comments like those you made during the operation give me no direction.

→ When you raise your voice to me in the operating room in front of all the staff, I feel embarrassed and humiliated. Those feelings make it difficult for me to focus on the surgery. If you have any negative feedback on my performance, I would appreciate it if you speak to me in private and give me specific recommendations on how I can improve.

If there is no satisfactory resolution to the conflict, the issue should be bumped up the chain of command.

A 79-year-old man is admitted to the intensive care unit (ICU) with suspected sepsis, dehydration, and tachycardia. The ICU resident and attending physician develop a plan for rehydration. The attending physician tells the resident not to administer any medications to slow down the patient's heart rate, as the intravenous (IV) fluids he is getting should treat the tachycardia. Later that night, the resident, noting that the patient still has a fast heart rate, orders a large dose of a beta-blocker to be administered to the patient. Twenty minutes later, the patient is found to be in cardiac arrest and dies.

This resident's actions likely had a significant role in this patient's death. The resident did not follow the strict recommendations of the attending physician. The resident needs to be firmly reprimanded for his actions. Even if his actions did not have such a bad outcome, they could in the future. When reprimanding a resident, be sure that your remarks are non-derisive and constructive. An example of an abusive remark is:

➔ You are an idiot. You purposely disobeyed me, and now you've killed this patient. How can you even call yourself a doctor?

You don't want the reprimand to be abusive, but it must be clear that the resident has been insubordinate and acted in an unsafe manner. A better way to reprimand the resident is:

➔ I am very angry that you changed our treatment plan without consulting with me first. I have the ultimate responsibility for this patient. When you are on this ICU service, I am your boss and you need to follow the directions that I give and discuss any changes in the treatment plan with me directly.

A surgical resident is called to the ED to repair a leg wound that an older woman sustained during a fall. The resident requests that an electrocautery device be brought down from the operating room for the repair. The nurse taking care of the patient is not familiar with the device and does not want the resident to use it in the ED.

→ <u>To the nurse:</u> I'm the doctor here, and I don't care what you want. Just go and get me that machine, and power it up.

This aggressive response to the nurse's concerns will not clear up the conflict. A much more constructive way to deal with the conflict is to address the reasons behind the conflict.

→ What are your concerns about using this device in the ED?

→ We haven't used this device in the ED before. Is it safe to use down here? I don't want the nursing staff or the patient to get electrocuted.

By addressing the reasons behind the conflict instead of barking orders, the resident got to the heart of the conflict—the nurse's valid concerns about staff and patient safety.

→ Thanks for looking out for the patient's safety. This device is very safe. It has a special grounding pad that prevents electrical shocks to the patient and to the people around the patient. Let me show you how it works.

While on rounds, an internal medicine resident is examining an ulcer on a patient's sacrum. The resident doesn't believe that the nurse dressed the wound properly. The attending physician, two medical students, the nurse, and the patient's family are in the room at this time.

→ <u>To the nurse, in front of everyone else in the room:</u> What have you done here? This is a really poor wound dressing. We are trying to make this wound get better, not worse.

A sarcastic and nasty comment like this is not constructive in any way. It is never appropriate to argue with or disparage a colleague up or down the chain of command in front of patients. If there are disagreements between healthcare professionals, they should be discussed in private away from patients. The attending physician should take the resident aside in private and address his or her behavior.

→ I noticed that you got pretty upset with the nurse in that last patient's room. I know that you care about this patient and have been working very hard to make sure he gets better. However, you should have handled that differently.

Try to give "real-time" feedback on behavioral issues to your colleagues. If a resident or nurse is having behavioral issues or multiple conflicts with coworkers, an attending physician or nurse manager, respectively, should discuss these issues with him or her as soon as possible. Letting conflicts drag out or fester can allow them to worsen.

→ I don't want to see you talk to the nursing staff that way and especially not in front of patients. You make all of us look incompetent when you do that. We are all on the same "team" here. If you don't think that the nurse is dressing the wound correctly, tell her in private.

Another way to make the same point is:

→ I'm a little concerned about your behavior. You seem to have a short fuse during rounds, and you really let loose on that nurse. Is there anything bothering you here at work or at home? Is there anything we can do to help you?

A nurse is checking the surgical site on a patient who has recently had a cesarean section. She needs to change the dressing but would like the resident to see the wound before she covers it back up. The obstetrics resident is making rounds on all of the post-operative patients on the unit.

→ The patient in room 708 needs her wound checked so that I can change the dressing. I really need to move on to my other patients, but I have to finish with this patient first. Can't you just come and examine her now so that I can get the rest of my work done?

→ Why are you bothering me with these trivial problems? Can't you see that I am busy with rounds? I'll get to it when I have time.

All members of the healthcare team have important duties. It's important to consider the priorities and workload of other team members. In this situation, both the nurse and the resident are more focused on their own priorities. They could both try to compromise to meet each other's needs.

➜ I know you are busy with rounds, but it would be helpful to me and the patient if you could just "eyeball" her wound. That way I can finish dressing her wound, and you could finish the rest of her assessment later.

➜ I'm sorry, but I am too busy right now. If you dress the wound, I promise that I will take care of redressing it once I come back to examine the patient. That way you won't have to dress the wound twice and can move on to your other patients.

A nurse has just had a new patient assigned to her treatment area on a medical floor. The patient was admitted with diverticulitis but did complain of chest pain to the nurse as she was being assessed. The nurse has called the on-call physician three times to tell her about the patient's chest pain.

➜ Dr. Lo, I've called you several times now about Mrs. Goss's chest pain. When are you going to order pain medicines and some cardiac labs?

➜ The patient didn't tell me about any chest pain. I did not get that from history taking, and what I got is all that counts.

The physician is being condescending toward the nurse and, in doing so, is also ignoring the patient's care and safety. Even if the physician doesn't agree with the nurse's assessment, she should acknowledge the nurse's concerns and address the possible medical issue with the patient.

→ Thanks for being concerned about this patient. When I admitted her, I really had no concerns about cardiac disease. I'll come up to see her shortly and decide about pain medicines and cardiac testing then.

Bluntly ignoring the concerns of a member of the medical team can create an atmosphere of tension or underappreciation. This may lead to that team member hesitating to bring up patient safety concerns in the future.

A patient has just been admitted to a bed on a medical unit. The unit secretary is with the patient and collecting his health insurance information. This information must be entered into the computer system before orders can be placed for the patient. The patient's physician has come to see the patient before she goes on rounds.

Healthcare professionals must work with all types of ancillary staff, such as custodians and clerical staff. It can be easy to look down on ancillary staff because they are not directly involved in patient care. Yet, their work is vital to keeping any hospital or medical practice running smoothly and safely.

→ <u>To the unit secretary:</u> I'm very busy and need to examine this patient right away. You need to hold off with your paperwork until I'm done.

→ I'm almost done with this paperwork. You'll just have to wait until I'm finished with my job. You can't even put in orders until I'm done anyway.

Although there are competing priorities here, it is clear that each healthcare worker has a vital role in the patient's care. They need to voice the importance of their respective tasks in a professional manner and must try to work together. A better exchange is:

→ I really need to talk with the patient first. Her care cannot proceed until I get this vital information into the computer. Is it all right for me to proceed?

→ The patient appears to be in some distress. Please let me ask a few key questions so that I have an idea of where she stands. After that, I'll let you finish your paperwork, and I'll get more information from the patient later.

CHAPTER 7

Perfect Phrases for Dealing with Difficult Administrative Staff

I n the United States, there is a growing trend of doctors moving from private practice to hospital-based practices. According to the American Medical Association, in 2009, one in six doctors worked for hospitals. This trend is driven by the economics of contemporary healthcare, as more and more doctors find it economically unfeasible to run a private practice. There are many benefits to hospital-based practices, such as improved tracking of patient records and better access to sub-specialists.

Yet, working for a hospital or a large healthcare provider, such as a health maintenance organization (HMO), places healthcare professionals under the authority of administrative management. The majority of administrative managers have very little, if any, background in the sciences or medicine. They may have degrees in management or business, and their "bottom line" is likely financial in nature. Administrators must ensure that the hospital complies with national and state-wide standards, such as Medicare Hospital Compare. Conversely, physicians often have little background or education in business or management principles and may not adequately understand the motivations of an administrator.

The "bottom line" for us as physicians and healthcare professionals should always be what is best for our patients. As we move toward hospital-based practices, we will have to manage relationships with administrative staff, who may have different priorities. Working well with colleagues on the administrative side of the hospital contributes to a better work environment and can hopefully lead to resource allocation and policies that benefit our patients in the end.

Perfect Phrases for Administrators Upset About Delays in Patient Care

Administrators are often the first hospital representatives to field patient complaints. One of the most common patient complaints has to do with delays in care. Unfortunately, delays in patient care are commonplace in busy hospitals. A packed Emergency Department (ED) can force patients to sit for hours in a crowded waiting room. When a hospital is fully occupied, it may lead to delays in finding a room for admitted patients. Delays in the operating room (OR) can leave patients languishing in the pre-operative or post-operative areas.

Administrators will bring the complaints that they have fielded back to the department or to the individuals involved in the incidents. Although we, as healthcare professionals, are concerned with providing top-quality medical care, delays in patient care can have negative effects on patient outcomes. Do not allow your interactions with administrative staff to become antagonistic or contentious. Instead, work with administrative staff to improve bottlenecks in patient care.

The Emergency Department (ED) at City Hospital has had increasingly long wait times. The hospital chief executive officer (CEO) has requested a meeting with the ED chairwoman and has brought along a list of patient complaints related to wait times.

→ We have logged an increasing number of complaints from patients about delays in care in the ED. Some patients have said that they will never come back to our hospital again. How could you let all these delays occur?

Delays in patient care are not always due to situations over which you, your department, or your hospital has direct control. When addressing delays with administrators, take a genuine interest in helping to fix the issues that you can control. Try not to view concerns from administrative staff as personal affronts against your work ethic or clinical skills. Maintain a forward-thinking attitude, and use some of the following phrases when discussing problems areas.

➜ I'm sorry to hear about all of the recent complaints. I don't believe that the delays are something that we intentionally let occur. However, I do recognize that there is a problem, and I'll be happy to talk about ways to fix the problem.

➜ I will be happy to go through these complaints and directly contact the patients who were upset. However, I don't think that all of the delays in patient care can be directly attributed to policies or problems in the ED itself. I want to fix this problem, too. Let's set up a meeting to explore the root causes of the delays and come up with solutions together.

Acknowledge the administrator's concerns, but be sure to focus the discussion on solutions to problems rather than on compiling a list of shortcomings.

The Operating Room (OR) at Suburban Hospital has had to cancel a number of surgical cases due to delays. The hospital CEO has requested a meeting with the chairwoman of the Department of Surgery.

Administrators often lack a medical background, and their work environment is often an office with regular hours. As a result, they may not understand the multifactorial nature of problems that we, as healthcare professionals, have to deal with in clinical settings. Instead of having them monitor and critique your hard work from an office, bring them to your department to let them see firsthand what you have to deal with on a daily basis.

→ Thanks for bringing these delays to my attention. We have also been keeping track of the problem and would like to solve it. Why don't you come spend a few hours with us in the OR? I'd like to show you firsthand some of the issues we encounter.

When the administrators are present, take the time to tell them about your typical day. Use real, live events to illustrate how your area works and why certain problems arise.

→ Housekeeping is one area that slows us down. You can see here that we have four ORs that still need to be cleaned. Once those rooms are cleaned, we could put four surgical cases into them. But as you can see, we don't have enough custodial staff to get this done. Can you help us get some additional custodians on busy days?

When you show an administrator some of the problems first-hand, they become more invested in finding a realistic solution to the problem.

Perfect Phrases for Administrators Wanting Special Treatment for Certain Patients

Administrative staff may ask us to provide expedited or preferred treatment for hospital VIPs (very important persons). Sometimes, these VIPs are politicians, donors to the hospital, or even family members of administrators.

A friend of a member of the hospital board of trustees has developed chest pain. The board member has called a cardiologist at the hospital and has asked that his friend be admitted to the hospital for testing and monitoring. However, the inpatient beds at the hospital are almost completely full, and there are several patients waiting in the clinic and in the ED for beds.

There are ethical issues associated with providing preferential treatment to certain patients over others. If you do "pull some strings" for a VIP, it should not jeopardize the care of other patients. The sickest patients should always come first, regardless of whether or not they are a VIP.

→ Thanks for calling to tell us about your friend. I need to let you know that the hospital is almost full and we have several very sick patients in the cardiac unit that I need to attend to first. What I can do is have the charge nurse keep an eye out for your friend. When he gets here, she will alert me. I will let him know that we don't have a bed for him right this minute. While we are looking for a bed for him, I will have the nurses draw blood for some tests and get an electrocardiogram (ECG).

The board member calls the cardiologist to make sure that his friend has arrived safely. The board member also asks about his friend's test results.

The *Health Insurance Portability and Accountability Act (HIPAA)* laws clearly dictate what medical information can be shared and with whom. If the patient has not given his express approval, you cannot discuss any details of his care with a friend.

➜ Thanks for calling to check up on your friend. We were able to find a bed for him and are evaluating his chest pain right now. He is stable, but I can't tell you much more than that until I get his permission to let you know about his results. I know that he is a good friend of yours, but I'm sure that you remember the hospital across town that got fined for not following privacy laws.

Perfect Phrases for Conflicts with Administrators over Allocation of Resources

Administrators are tasked with balancing the books and thus may have a mind-set that is focused on the bottom line. As healthcare professionals, we must keep our patients' best interests in mind but also be mindful that financial resources are limited and should be directed to areas that can do the most good for our patients.

The Department of Radiology has requested that the hospital purchase a new computed tomography (CT) scanner. The newer model is faster and produces higher-resolution images. However, it is very expensive and will use a significant portion of the annual budget for equipment purchases.

When making proposals for expenditure of capital to administrators, remember to "speak their language." A person without a medical background won't necessarily understand the medical and financial benefits of a device with a higher sensitivity or better resolution.

➜   This new CT scanner will cost a lot of money, but it will make our department more efficient because we will be able to scan more patients in a shorter time. I think the higher-resolution images can lead to more accurate diagnoses. The higher accuracy should also lead to decreased malpractice cases. These factors should help us bring in more money to the hospital.

Try using some of the phrases below when asking for resources to be dedicated to an area you think is important.

→ I know that this new antibiotic is more expensive than the one we currently have on formulary. But this new one has a broader coverage. With a broader coverage antibiotic, we can get people treated and discharged from the hospital faster and improve our patient throughput. I think this can save the hospital money in the long run.

→ This new Foley catheter is coated with a silver compound. The silver coating makes the device more expensive, but I have a research paper I can show you that proves that using this product decreases costs overall because it significantly reduces the chances of a patient getting a urinary infection.

→ We can make do for now with the old computer system. However, this may lose us money in the long run, as we will miss out on billing opportunities that the new system can automatically track for us.

→ I understand that resources are limited. However, our current ultrasound machine doesn't give us the best images. I strongly feel that this new machine is vital to improving our patient care, and I cannot provide the best care without it. Could we explore options to help fund it?

→ I recognize that this new blood testing machine will cost a lot to purchase and maintain, but in the long run, having the ability to run this test will save us money on malpractice costs. In addition, I've noted that a lot of patients are asking if we do this test. We could lose revenue to other hospitals that do this test if we don't have this machine.

The Orthopedics Department (OD) at a community hospital is looking to expand its office space. It would like to take over the offices used by Internal Medicine (IM) for a clinic that serves low-income patients from the neighborhoods near the hospital. The chair of IM is meeting with the hospital's CEO.

➔ As you know, the OD would like to expand into the space used for your clinic. The OD is the most profitable department at this hospital, and I think their growth is important to the overall growth of the hospital.

➔ I understand your point of view, and I recognize that the hospital must keep its finances in order. However, we do provide a significant amount of care to local patients at a low cost. Obviously, we do not bring in as much money to the hospital as the OD does, but we do provide an important community service.

➔ Your doctors and nurses do great work in the clinic, but I have to focus on the financial aspects of running this hospital, too.

➔ I think we should also consider the mission statement of the hospital. It states that our priorities are "Quality and Safe Patient Care, Employee Development, and Hospital Finances." I agree that we do have to factor care for the needy into our balance sheets. But the clinic really brings this hospital a lot of goodwill and positive local press and is in keeping with the mission statement. Could we work together to find another space for the OD or find some money in the budget to fund running our clinic elsewhere in the hospital?